Here now in love

Pg 10

Other books by Philip St. Romain
from Liguori Publications

Caring for the Self, Caring for the Soul:
A Book of Spiritual Development, 2000

Praying the Daily Gospels:
A Guide to Meditation, 1995

Reflecting on the Serenity Prayer, 1997

With Lisa Bellecci-st. Romain

Living Together, Loving Together:
A Spiritual Guide to Marriage

The Roots of Contemplative Spirituality

Here now in love

Philip St. Romain

Liguori/Triumph
LIGUORI, MISSOURI

Imprimi Potest:
Richard Thibodeau, C.Ss.R.
Provincial, Denver Province
The Redemptorists

Published by Liguori/Triumph
An imprint of Liguori Publications
Liguori, Missouri
www.liguori.org
www.catholicbooksonline.com

Library of Congress Cataloging-in-Publication Data

St. Romain, Philip A.
    Here now in love : the roots of contemplative spirituality / Philip St. Romain.—1st ed.
        p. cm.
    ISBN 0-7648-0793-5 (pbk.)
    1. Spiritual life—Catholic Church. I. Title.

BX2350.65 S73 2002
248.4'82—dc21   2001038558

Printed in the United States of America
06 05 04 03 02   5 4 3 2 1
First edition

*F*or several years, Phil St. Romain has used the e-mail signature, "Be here now in love and all shall be well." Obviously, this book has been germinating within him for a long time. The mystic, Julian of Norwich, tells us that one loving blind desire for God is more helpful to our friends than anything else we could do.

As I relate to Phil at the Heartland Center for Spirituality, I find that his blind desire for God encourages me to be here now in love. Undoubtedly, you are also on this journey or you wouldn't be pursuing this book right now!

If you reflectively ponder the text, and faithfully engage in the suggested practices, you will grow more peacefully centered in the now and, as well, more trusting and courageous in love. Phil St. Romain speaks the language of the twenty-first century seeker while teaching the wisdom of the great spiritual masters.

LOUISE HAGEMAN, OP

Contents

Part Two:
Practices That Promote Freedom
to Live in the Here and Now 53

Introduction

❧

*D*uring the past two decades, spirituality has become a very popular topic. Once the exclusive province of the religions of the world, it has "broken free" from that connection. Many people see spirituality as something that is superior, or more life-giving, which appears to be in opposition to religious traditions. Today, it is common to hear people say that they are spiritual, but not religious—an affirmation that would have appeared to be an oxymoron in decades past. At the same time, there are numerous "churchgoers" who state that although they are content with the teachings of their particular tradition, they just don't find much "life" in them. We might say that they are religious people in search of a deeper spirituality.

What do we mean by the term "spirituality"? From my perspective, spirituality refers to something that brings a sense of meaning, centeredness, energy, and self-transcendence to a person. Taken in this light, we can assert that every human being already has a certain spirituality, for we are all spiritual beings seeking to give our lives that aforementioned sense of meaning, centeredness, and energy at the same time as we search for ways to go beyond ourselves in ecstasy. For example, spirituality may present itself in various forms: for some, it's in their job; countless others look to a special human relationship. Alcohol, drugs, gambling, sex, and other such dependencies could also constitute spiritualities when our attachment to them grows to the extent that these dependencies begin to define who we are and what we do.

The question, then, is not whether a person has a type of spirituality, but what their spirituality really is. In other words, "what makes you tick"? Why do you get up in the morning and do what you do? What gives you meaning for your life and makes you happy, and how do you pursue this? Your answers to these questions begin to reveal your spirituality.

This book was written in an attempt to articulate a contemplative Christian spirituality. As such, it draws on the treasures of the Christian tradition while making use, at times, of the contemporary gifts available to us from psychology and Eastern religious traditions. The fundamental premise of Christian spirituality is that the God who was revealed to us by Jesus Christ is a God of love who is available to us every second of every day. Furthermore, the spirituality suggested by this theological conviction is one that implies that if we are to know God, we must be where he is, or we will miss him. We must strive to be like God, or we will not be able to recognize God. In other words, we must be in the right place, at the right time, in the right way: we must *be here now in love.*"

This spirituality is not a new one, Christian saints and mystics and, indeed, the members of all the world's religions have lived it throughout time. It describes our common vocation: to love God with our whole heart, soul, mind, and strength, and our neighbor (including creation) as ourselves. The lifestyle one chooses—be it married, celibate, religious, or so on—will depend upon a person's own unique gifts and the particular graces which draw him or her down the pathway of loving now. Thus, this spirituality does not have the intention of supplanting the many wonderful spiritualities which have arisen in the Church (Carmelite, apostolic, lay, and so forth), but to show what they all have in common at their root.

Therefore, dear reader, it is my hope that no matter what stage you may find yourself at on life's spiritual journey, you will find this work useful. The process of writing and articulating this book has actually brought more depth and clarity to my own journey. As well, sharing it with other people by means of an Internet retreat has proven to me that it also works for others. Its simple format makes it easy even for a beginner to understand, and, at the same time, it has enough depth for those who are experienced travelers along the spiritual road.

Acknowledgments

I am most grateful to my wife, Lisa, for our marriage of twenty-four years. In her presence, I find it easy to be here now in love. My children have also helped this cerebral soul keep his feet on the ground while calling forth depths of love I would have never discovered without them. The team at Heartland Center for Spirituality provided support, encouragement, and helpful feedback during the writing process. And the fifty or so participants in the Internet retreat on this topic helped to clarify many of the teachings offered here.

It would take pages and pages to thank the many authors and teachers who have contributed to this work. Some of the more significant contributors have been indicated in the suggested-reading section at the end of the book.

Finally, I would like to thank the staff at Liguori Publications for their encouragement to continue working at this project even when I had given up on it.

PHILIP ST. ROMAIN

Part One

Living and Loving
in the Here and Now

*D*uring the past twenty-seven years, I have made a serious study of Christian spirituality and attempted to put what I have learned into practice. Time and again, the same lessons have been impressed upon me, for, like so many others, I am slow to learn, and even more remiss when it comes to practicing what I know to be true. In times of clarity, I have, without confusion, seen the truth of "what it's all about," only to have my mind eventually move on to a search for "greater truths" through an endless series of "greener pastures" which, in the end, turned out to be dead-end streets paved with empty promises. I am, once again, led back to the basics, which, although not so terribly difficult to understand, do leave the unregenerate mind bored and unsatisfied. This "problem of the mind," I am happy to say, has also been revealed for what it truly is. At long last, even the mind is now prepared to affirm what the spirit has long recognized.

WHAT IS THE MESSAGE?

And what is this great lesson I have learned? Simply this: *life is a never-ending flow of opportunities from which to choose, yet the only choice which brings peace and happiness is to "be here now in love."*

I know this statement might sound simplistic, or even trite. Nevertheless, as well as being the spiritual message at the heart of all the world religions, it is also what brings unconditional happiness. These religions, with all their dogmas and rituals, are supposed to lead us to deeply embrace a life of being here now in love but, unfortunately, we also find many aspects of religion that distract us from this simple practice. These circumstances occur so frequently that it sometimes appears that religion itself can become an impediment to experiencing truth. I have fallen into this trap numerous times, and seen many others do the same. I have come to the conclusion that a religion that enables people to be here now in love is a good religion, while a religion that distracts one from this spirituality is bad—perhaps even to the extent of becoming an addictive involvement.

By speaking of this spirituality as a "practice," what I mean is that a person must not simply believe intellectually in its truth, he or she must also get involved and *do it*. Those who make even the smallest attempt at following this practice will immediately notice an increase in their sense of peace and inner harmony. They may also find that it is difficult to live consistently in this manner throughout the entire day. This difficulty may be evident to such an extent that even though practitioners conclude that living in the present moment in love is an interesting experience, they may also question if there isn't something more. Indeed, there *is* more: more confusion, running around in circles, and an endless number of ways to keep oneself upset, distracted, and out of touch with life. But just a few seconds of the experience of being here now in love can virtually redeem what would typically be labeled as a "bad day."

Of course, almost everything about this practice of "being here now in love" needs to be qualified and properly understood. What, for example, does it actually mean to "be here now"? Does it mean that one forgets the past, or makes no preparation for the future? And what do we mean by the word "love"? Goodness knows, we have all encountered the many aberrations of this word, so much so that we might even have come to despair that love is anything more than a subtle way people have of manipulating one another. In this book I will address some of these common misconceptions, all the while encouraging the reader to test what I say in the light of personal experience.

PUTTING THE MESSAGE INTO PRACTICE

Let's get going and give it a try! Starting right here and now, endeavor to live your life more attentively, be present to this moment and what is happening, both inside and outside of you. Let your awareness be gentle, soft, nonjudgmental (another word that needs to be qualified), and allow your will or intentionality to open itself to loving as best as you understand it is able. When you become confused about what love requires, pray for guidance, using simple prayers and phrases that come from your own heart. When your attention strays from this simple practice, gently bring it back and start over, taking note of what took you off track. Start over, again and again and again, rejoicing in the fact that it is possible to do so. With each new beginning, "present-moment loving" will become more deeply ingrained, and it will gradually become a habitual way of being. With consistent effort, it will become who you actually are. That is the point when you will know the true meaning of this passage of Scripture: "It is no longer I who live, but it is Christ who lives in me" (Gal 2:20).

PRAYER, CORNERSTONE OF OUR RELATIONSHIP WITH GOD

We become what we see. This spiritual law is an important one to remember. If you spend a great deal of time paying attention to television, it will certainly influence your development. If you spend an excessive amount of time at your computer screen, it may change your perspective on life. But what would happen if you spent more time attending to God? That's really what prayer is supposed to be about.

Simply put, *prayer is attending to God*, the One who is always present to you in love.

All through each and every day, you are invited to be lovingly attentive to God as you drive a car, talk with a coworker, do your work, and so forth. But in prayer, you drop everything except your loving attentiveness to God. By doing so, after you arise from prayer, you increase your capacity to be here now in love so that you are able to go out and do what needs to be done. The quality of your presence is thus formed and deepened in prayer. Without prayer, it would be difficult to be here now in love throughout the day.

What kind of prayer will do? Almost any kind of prayer will do, provided that the focus is on loving God, and being loved by God. It goes without saying that you couldn't have this focus if the majority of your time is spent in intercessory prayer, asking God for help for yourself or someone else. There is no problem with saying prayers such as these, but it is doubtful that you will deepen your love of God if that's the extent of your prayers.

TYPES OF PRAYER

There are two main types of prayer which are emphasized in all of the world religions. One of these is called *kataphatic prayer*. This prayer type refers to our seeking God through the means of certain familiar forms. Such prayer recognizes God to be a relational partner, and addresses God using various images and concepts. Included here is God's presence (to us) in the form of a person, Jesus. Praying with Scripture is also an example of kataphatic prayer, as is saying the rosary. By focusing on some "symbolic" representation of God's presence, you are thus able to direct your attention more fully to God, and will find God speaking to you using these means. Our human consciousness needs this kind of prayer, for it leaves us with a sense of "being in a relationship" with God. This sense of relationship will evoke an experience with God's love in which you are aware of your movements to conversion, and consciously seek a more intimate alliance with God through Christ so that you can serve him better.

The other prayer type is called *apophatic prayer*. It refers to prayer without the use of images. Here, you simply call to mind the concept that God's loving presence saturates all things. You enter into a general sense of attentiveness to God, opening your being to receive whatever God wants to give. You come to know God as the "ground" of your own being and the presence at the heart of all things. No words can adequately express this experience, so apophatic prayer emphasizes loving silence and "unknowing" as its distinctive features. You forget your own sense of self and concentrate your total attention on God's existence. This abandonment to God will evoke a union with him beyond our conscious awareness.

The Church has long recognized the validity of these two kinds of prayer, and, in my opinion, I believe a healthy spiritual life requires both. Generally speaking, it seems quite natural for us to use a kataphatic approach when beginning our prayers. We read Scripture, pray for our needs, and relate to God as "an-Other," or to Jesus, or to other intercessors. After some time, the presence of God, which transcends all concepts and images, leads us to the general loving attentiveness of apophatic, contemplative prayer. We might remain here for a while, returning to kataphatic prayer at a later time.

PUTTING PRAYER INTO PRACTICE

The most important thing is to take time each day to pray. If you are new to the spiritual life, I recommend at least two twenty-minute periods each day. If you're a seasoned veteran, then you know the importance of prayer, but perhaps you've lost the focus of using prayer time to be present to God. I've certainly had this happen in my own life. There have been days when, while in prayer, I spent a great deal of time meditating on the meaning of the Scripture, or praying for people on my prayer list, only to discover, after a while, that I was losing a sense of God's presence in my own life.

What I recommend is that you find an approach to prayer that works best for you, and then use it to give your full attention to God. Pray for your needs and for those of others: that's fine. But after that is done, just "look at God" and invite him to show you the way.

You will certainly discover that it is very difficult to give God your full, undivided attention for very long. Your mind will carry your focus away. Don't worry, everyone has this very same problem. It is only when apophatic contemplation becomes deeply established that you will find your mind become relatively quiet. When you find your mind wandering, just bring it back. You may even find that you will be doing this again and again. Use a simple key word such as "God" or "Jesus" to bring your attention back. Let this word be a verbal expression of your consent to God's will and his action within your being (this is sometimes called centering prayer).

Every time you choose to give your full attention to God rather than being distracted, you grow stronger spiritually. *Each and every time!* But take note, however, that I am making a distinction between being distracted and *getting involved with these distractions.* As we have already seen, you will surely be bothered by distractions, that's simply unavoidable. In a manner of speaking, each distraction "owns," as it were, a "piece" of your attention. When you give yourself over to a distraction, you give it more attention, more energy, and you become more involved in its agenda. When you note the distraction without getting caught up in it, turning your attention away from it and toward God (using a prayer word or a short intercessory prayer for the concern raised by the distraction), you give yourself over to God and become more like what you see, which is God. Also, your attention and energy become freed from the distraction itself. That little "piece" of yourself, which was out of your personal control, now becomes more integrated as a part of your true self.

Therefore, you must pray if you want to grow in the Spirit. No excuses! Get up earlier in the morning if you must. Let the primary focus of your prayer be on developing your conscious contact with God (Step Eleven of the Twelve Steps. See page 108). Don't determine the level of success of your prayer time according to the level of distractions you experienced. Sometimes, distractions signify that the Spirit is hard at work within you. Other times, you might find yourself so enraptured with God that you don't want to leave your prayer. Of course, that's good too! We need such times, or we would find ourselves getting discouraged. Please don't think your time has been wasted when that sense of being "lost in God" doesn't happen. As someone once said, the success of prayer is primarily evaluated according to one criterion: *you showed up!*

MIRACLE OF THE PRESENT MOMENT

One of my favorite stories from the Bible is Moses appearing before the burning bush. I am sure you've heard it, and maybe even seen it portrayed in the movies.

While tending a flock of sheep, up on the mountain, Moses saw that a bush was burning, but it was not being consumed by the fire. Deciding to examine it more closely, he approached it, and heard a voice which called out to him, "Moses! Moses!" He answered, "Here I am" (Ex 3:4). God tells Moses that he is on holy ground, and they enter into a discussion about liberating the Israelites from slavery in Egypt.

Moses' response, "Here I am," is of critical importance in this story. It could certainly be interpreted as a conversational courtesy, but I think it implies something more. "Here I am," in this case, can also mean "I am here." Because Moses was attentive to life, he noticed the burning bush, and was then able to be open to entering into its mystery. Throughout the rest of his life, he continued to manifest this sense of presence, through which, at times, the glory of God shone so brightly Moses had to put a veil over his face.

To *be here now* means to be present to what is happening at this moment, both within yourself and in the world around you. The reason this sense of "nowness" is important is because life is happening to you right now, and only now. What has happened in the past is done (although you may have memories), and what will happen in the future does not yet exist (except in your imagination). If you miss this moment, then you miss your life itself, and if you miss your life, what a tragedy!

Most people don't live in the now. Their consciousness is

divided between events in the past, and projections of events in the future. This generates a never-ending stream of preoccupying thoughts, concerns, anxieties, and plans, which drain one of energy and, as well, produce a feeling of alienation from God, others, and the whole of creation. The present moment comes and goes like a blurred light and is only fully entered into during extraordinary happenings or during intensely demanding circumstances. In order to maintain a "sense of life," one may waste a great deal of time and energy thinking about how to create or avoid such stimulating circumstances. And, during all of this time, life continues to present itself in each and every moment of the day, but, sadly, it is being missed.

Living in the now is also important because God is in the moment. It is true that God can be present to us through our memories or imaginations, but the intersection between eternity (God's time) and historical time is this present moment. God wants to break into human history now through every creature, but for this incarnation to take place within us, we must give our consent.

CLARIFYING THE PRACTICE OF BEING HERE NOW

Although being present to the moment might seem to be simple, there are many misconceptions. The following are a few I have seen and dealt with in my own life:

1. *To be present in the moment means you must concentrate hard on what's happening now.* Far from it! Intense concentration that is full of effort actually isolates you from the present moment and exhausts your mental and volitional resources. Instead, what is required is a more relaxed

and open attentiveness. Some have called this "looking softly" or "just-looking." In such attentiveness, you're simply observing what is happening. The fruit of this "seeing" is a clarity of perception.

2. *To be present in the moment means you must analyze what is happening here and now.* Not at all. This, too, will exhaust your resources and may actually take you out of the present moment. Analysis draws the attention into the operations of the intellect, which are one or more steps removed from the present moment. This is not to say that life does not sometimes call for such intellectual activity: it does, and when this happens, you have to use your intellect to either solve problems or critically examine your options. But 95 percent of the things you do each day don't call for such analytical activity.

3. Another distorted idea is that *living in the present moment means forgetting the past and making no plans for the future.* Again, there are certain circumstances when you have to do both, but these constitute only a small percentage of situations you encounter. My experience has been that when you are living attentively the lessons of the past are still there. They arise to serve the needs of the moment when it is appropriate. This happens quite effectively—much more often than when I am living in a state of analytical or emotional preoccupation. The same sort of process happens with respect to the future. While living attentively, I see how what is happening right now may have ramifications for the future or how I need to prepare for the future in this present moment. This approach is quite different from living *in* the past or *in* the future, which is, usually, an escape mechanism. But if focused remembering or deliberate planning is needed, that's fine too!

4. *Only certain personality types can live in the present moment.* It is true that sensate personality types (those who are captivated with things that can be experienced through a sense modality), as described by Jung and other notable psychologists, are more naturally focused on the "here and now" details of life, but attentiveness to the moment is much more than this. Sensate types can be excessively overly absorbed in details without being very attentive to either themselves or to life. The same may hold for any other personality type. Present-moment living calls for a relaxed, global attentiveness that encompasses all the activities of the mind and senses. When attention is operating primarily in only one or two of the functions (thinking, feeling, sensation, intuition), the other functions and more subtle levels of intelligence are deprived of additional resources in forming a response to the moment.

5. *If I am present to the moment without analyzing it, or exerting myself through my will, how will I know what to do?* You already possess, within yourself, the skills needed to do thousands of tasks without thinking about each of them separately. In fact, it would probably do you a great deal of good to try to do a few things each day without actually thinking specifically about them. Once learned through attention, study, and practice, skills-intelligence is stored in the memory and will be available when needed. This kind of "doing" is not, in any way, irresponsible or unconscious if you are living attentively while you are doing it. "Do what you're doing" is a good affirmation to use to bring yourself to this kind of presence. If, however, you choose to do one thing (for instance, drive your car) while thinking about another (a forthcoming meeting at work), that's fine. Just be aware of what you're doing and take responsibility for it.

6. *If I'm not critically analyzing what's happening in the present moment, how will I know what to do? And doesn't this open the door to immoral behavior?* These questions have more to do with your responsiveness to the moment rather than with what attentive living is—a matter which I will discuss at length in the following pages. For now, however, I do want to emphasize that if you are not living in the present moment, then responsiveness to the needs of the moment is a moot point.

PUTTING PRESENT-MOMENT LIVING INTO PRACTICE

There is nothing very complicated here! Keep it simple. *Just let your attention be relaxed, aware, and globally present to what's going on within and around you.* Just take a look around. Take time to see and observe what is there. This point has been discussed previously, but now you know more about what this practice entails or does not entail.

Here is an important key: follow the lead of the physical body! The human body is always in the right place at the right time: here and now. When our attention is caught up with mental and emotional preoccupations, however, we tend to lose touch with our body. The move to return to the present moment can, therefore, be enhanced by the action of attending to the reality/physicality of the body and its sensations, and even to its wisdom.

Be aware of what it feels like to be here now in the physical body. How does that feel? Take special notice of your breathing. Is it shallow, deep, choppy, or smooth? Allowing your awareness to become more open and global, just follow your breathing for a short time. If distractions persist, try doing ten-by-ten breathing: inhale deeply to a count of ten; hold that breath for ten seconds; exhale to a count of ten. Do this ten times, and you your awareness will become clearer and less preoccupied.

CULTIVATING INNER SILENCE

Many years ago, I decided to make a silent, directed eight-day retreat. I was still relatively new to the life of faith as an adult, but I wanted to do everything possible to deepen my relationship with God. An older friend had just returned from a similar retreat and told me how deeply he now experienced God's presence. My wife graciously agreed to be the single parent for our two young daughters in my absence. (I would later reciprocate.)

Full of fervor and anticipation, I arrived at the Jesuit Retreat Center in Grand Côteau, Louisiana. The grounds were beautiful; ancient oak trees laden with Spanish moss were situated across the property. The meals were superb, my room small and cozy, the liturgies well done, and my retreat director was a very wise religious sister. One might assume that all was going well, but this was not the case! I felt as if I were going crazy! Unaccustomed to s uch silence, my mind was constantly awhirl, and that was extremely frustrating! Living a lifestyle filled with hours of television, radio, movies, reading, and other "noise" had done more damage to my psyche than I had realized. I couldn't stop the thinking process and just "be," as my retreat director encouraged.

It took four days before I began to notice things slowing down inside and was able to look at the trees without thinking about a hundred other things at the same time. My prayers began to deepen as well, and I started to enjoy the simplicity of just being with God in loving silence, a type of contemplation. I felt more like myself—whole, peaceful, alive—than I had ever felt in my life! I resolved, if possible, to live on this level for the rest of my life. By the time the retreat had ended, I felt as if I was just beginning to become acclimated to the silence, and I dreaded my return to "normal life."

Upon my return, one of the first changes I made was to initiate a "media fast." Whereas before my retreat I needed to have either the radio or TV turned on at all times during the day and night, just to "keep up with things" (including the latest top forty hits), I began to leave things turned off unless I was really listening or watching. No more "background noise"! I read neither newspapers nor any magazines before morning prayer, and discovered that this, alone, helped me continue to deepen the interior silence that had begun within me on the retreat. On the days when I did listen to more radio or watch more TV, I noticed that my mind was definitely "noisier," and it was difficult to give my full attention to God in prayer.

Through the years, I have continued this media fast, adding video movies, e-mail, and Internet web surfing to the list of information resources that I utilize with discretion. It's not that I think there is anything inherently wrong with these technologies; it's just that they have to be used with care. It is the same for books, magazines, and newspapers. We live in what many call the "Information Age," and that is wonderful! But we must be made aware that all of the information which flows into our minds has a certain effect on us; it produces certain results, and we have to take responsibility for these outcomes.

KEEPING THE MIND IN CHECK

If you have been following along with the spirituality emphasized in this book, you have certainly come to experience its primary obstacle: *the noisy mind*. I have referred to this several times, including the account of my own retreat and post-retreat experiences.

One of the first things we need to realize is that the human brain and its interior mind did not evolve within the context of the Information Age. It evolved within the context of the natural environment, whose sounds it finds more soothing and calming. The information explosion of the past few decades is a new phenomenon, and we do not yet know how we shall emerge from it. Also unknown are the long-term consequences of our extended exposure to radio and television waves, microwaves, and other such invisible forces and how they affect the brain.

Based upon my own personal experience, as well as data gathered through meetings with many people for spiritual direction through the years, I can certainly affirm that all of this information to which we are exposed to seems to have a fragmenting effect on the psyche. Everything which comes into the psyche through the senses has to be processed, and when so much is coming in, compensation is made in order to reduce our sensitivity to the outside world. The result is that we then become numb to external signals, and we require more intense, more graphic doses of stimulation in order to override this acquired insensitivity and begin to feel anything.

Another observation is that much of the information we absorb promotes selfishness and materialism. The affective tone of messages on billboards, radio advertisements, and TV commercials suggests that the products being sold are important—even essential to life and even to our happiness! Rationally, we might reject this, but the emotional level of our being has its own intelligence, to which media advertisers are keenly attuned. Research has also shown the people who watch a great deal of TV believe the world to be more dangerous than those who watch less: they have more anxiety in their lives.

If you become more spiritually awake, you will come to see how your mind reacts to the information you put into it, and you must take full responsibility for doing something about this information overload. Take note of how you feel after you watch a movie, or listen to the radio. What's going on in your inner self after you view a TV program? Are you using these various media to escape contact with your inner self? Do you feel more alive, or more fragmented and numb? Are you more disposed to love and praise God? Are you more patient with family members?

These are the critical questions to the spiritual life. There is no more practical way to evaluate them than to try to be here now in love and watch what happens. If your mind keeps pulling your attention into different directions, then you need to find the reason why, and do something about it. The best context in which to learn about this is silence.

PUTTING THE ART OF SILENCE INTO PRACTICE

Here are a few tips to get you started:

- Initiate your own media fast. Abstain from all media (or as much as you can) for a week, then gradually reintroduce only those aspects that are informative, educational, and/or entertaining in an energizing way.
- Become more aware of the reasons you watch TV, listen to the radio, surf the Internet, and so forth. Ask yourself what needs you are trying to meet through them, and be honest with your answer. Be especially aware when you are indulging in these activities because you are bored, lonely, or the like. What else could you do to fulfill these needs? Why not take

some time for prayer and ask God to fulfill them for you?

- Notice how the media affects your mental and emotional processes. Keep a journal about this.
- Seriously observe the Sabbath. Let it become a day of rest, silence, and peace.
- Do what is fun, recreative, and what feeds your spirit.
- Spend more time outdoors, listening to the sounds of nature.
- Look up the retreat centers in your area and schedule a retreat. Most will allow you to go on your own private or self-directed retreat for short periods of time. And even if it's just a half day, you will find that this will help to renew your spirit.

OUR BODY, A GIFT

When I discover that I've become caught up in some type of drama pertaining to the past or the future, one of my favorite ways to refocus is to ask myself where my body is! I know this must sound pretty silly, but there's a profound truth here: *the body is always living in the present moment.* It cannot be anywhere else! It is our mind that jumps from the past to the future, and gets entangled in emotional, imaginative, or analytical preoccupations. When this happens, our attention gets caught up in our thoughts and we lose our consciousness of the body. The shortest way back into the here and now is by attentiveness to our body.

Christian spirituality hasn't always been kind toward the body. We've interpreted scriptural teachings about the Spirit being at enmity with the flesh to mean that there is something wrong with the body and its desires. Some erroneous, but popular, theological trends also maintained that matter and, therefore, the body, was inherently evil. But the real meaning of the Incarnation was that God became human. He took on human flesh! He had a body just like our own! Incarnational spirituality means that we, too, are called to let the Spirit radiate within our bodies. This is a gift!

Metaphysically, what we can affirm is that the body is the physical vehicle through which the spiritual soul expresses itself. In fact, we might even say that the body and the soul are not separate entities at all—as though you could have a body without a soul, or vice versa. When we die, our soul lives on, but the Church teaches that it is metaphysically deficient without a body. Thus, the soul will eventually be reunited with a body in the general resurrection of the dead. It will be clothed in a resurrected body that will respond fully to the Spirit working in the soul.

When we become estranged from our bodies through dislike, distrust, or even outright rejection, we become alienated from our souls as well. In this situation, it is also impossible to be here now in love, for the mind is constantly trying to determine how to live while, simultaneously, denying its full expression through the body. For example, we want to show love, but believe we are not attractive; we want to eat, but believe we're too fat; we want to dance, but believe we're too awkward. Even married couples have trouble celebrating their love openly and joyously through their sexuality due to a wide variety of "hang-ups" that fall into this category.

No matter what your physical appearance or state of health may be, it is possible for you to become friendlier terms with your body. The first step in caring for its needs is to regard it with unconditional love and acceptance, like a cherished gift. You don't have to settle for being overweight and out of shape, but you don't have to reject your body as you work with it to make a change. As you begin to love it better, you will find yourself beginning to do more of the positive things it needs.

TUNING IN TO THE SENSES

There are tens of thousands of nerve endings in the body—all of which are capable of giving us feedback and information about life as it is happening here and now. Some of these sensations are painful, but so many of them are enjoyable, such as

- the feel of the sunshine on your face when you are outside
- the smell of the air when you walk into your home
- the sound of the breeze blowing through the trees
- the taste of a really good meal

So many of us go through our days without noticing these simple pleasures! That is why we need stronger and stronger stimulation in order to experience our lives.

But if we begin to tune in to the simple sensory experiences available to us all day long, we will begin to live more fully in our body. We will also become more calm, for the mind will become more grounded in the here-and-now facts of life, and less preoccupied with other issues.

Once, a woman who was suicidal came to see me. Her husband had just left her, she had lost her job, and she felt hopeless. I listened for a while, convinced that I needed to get her into counseling somewhere soon, but she was too upset to even hear anything about this. Out of the blue, I had an inspiration. I asked her to stop and take a few deep breaths, and, at the same time, I asked the Spirit to be with us. I then asked her to look at the carpet in my office and tell me what colors she saw (it was a blend of many). She did this for some time, and then I asked her to tell me what shapes she saw (the pattern flowed in and out of a variety of images). She pointed out several. I then asked her how she felt, and she said she felt OK. "What kind of trick have you played on me?" she asked. "What's in that carpet?" I told her there was nothing magical about the carpet, but she had calmed down because she had brought her attention more into the here and now instead of obsessing about the past and projecting tragedy into the future. I went on to explain to her that she would have to learn to live like this—one moment at a time—and as time went on, she would be taken out of that painful past into a different future. "What you call the future is nothing but more present moments down the road, no different, in any way, from the ones you're experiencing now. Only *you* will be different." I gave her the names and phone numbers of a couple of good counselors and wished her well.

Although I never heard from her again, her visit helped to deeply impress upon me the power of present-moment awareness of sensory information to calm the mind and emotions.

OUR SENSES AND SPIRITUALITY

In his delightful book *The Song of the Bird*, Jesuit spiritual writer Anthony de Mello tells the following story:

> *The constant complaint of the disciple to his Zen Master was, "You are hiding the final secret of Zen from me." And he refused to believe the Master's denials.*
> *The Master one day took him for a walk along the hills. While they were walking, they heard a bird sing.*
> *"Did you hear that bird sing?" said the Master.*
> *"Yes," said the disciple.*

"Well, now you know that I have hidden nothing from you," said the Master.
"Yes," said the disciple.

He had heard the bird, and heard it *as* the bird. That was all, and it was enough!

Jesus also tells us to look at the birds of the sky, and the flowers of the field (see Mt 6:25–30). From them, we are to learn the lessons of simplicity and trust. But there is more! He tells us that "even Solomon in his regalia was not robed like one of these."

All creation springs fresh from the hand of God in each and every second. The Hindus like to say that God dances creation; to simply behold creation without judging, and without imposing our preconceptions upon it, is to behold something of the Dancer. Everything reveals God in some way, but we must be aware of it in order to be able to experience its blessings. Living with our senses open to these experiences can help us become more attuned to God's presence in all of creation and to our spirituality.

PUTTING BODILY AWARENESS INTO PRACTICE

Become aware of what it's like to be here now in the body. How does that feel? What are your senses telling you?

Take the time and stop during your various daily activities to simply scan your body and notice its sensations:

- the feel of your feet in your shoes
- how your clothing feels on your body
- the smell of the air around you
- the sounds in the air

Welcome these and other sensations that come into your awareness. Give thanks to God for the grace to be alive in your body, his gift. Give thanks for your senses.

THE ATTITUDE OF WILLINGNESS

If you have been attempting to practice what we have been discussing so far, being here in the now, you surely have discovered that your mind and attention may frequently become derailed by a wide variety of distracting concerns or preoccupations. Rest assured, this situation is not your fault! Don't feel badly about it! This is simply an example of how your mind has been conditioned over the years, and is not something you have consciously chosen to have happen. For now, simply consider this state of being preoccupied as a consequence of growing up in a world of conditional love. Note the sense of "brokenness" that the experience of conditional love has caused within you.

There are many types of preoccupations; they are not all negative. What I mean by the term "preoccupations," in this context, refers to the spontaneous, involuntary activities (thinking, emoting, having desires) that go on in your mind. They seem to just spontaneously happen: almost as if they have a will of their own. And, in fact, they *do* have a will of their own. They have been triggered by a wide variety of internal questions and beliefs that have been deeply implanted in your mind. Every time you act on these thoughts, you give them more energy, more "will."

Let me explain a little further. If one of my beliefs is that *in order for me to feel good about myself, other people must like me for myself*, then my mind will constantly be involved in evaluating whether the people around me seem to like me. I will constantly be involved in exploring ways to get others to like me more, even when they're not around. Here, my mind is working like a computer as it attempts to solve a problem. Every time I act on one of its suggestions, I give more of my attention and energy to the programming I have just reinforced. In time, this particular program will seem to be acting on its own, without my consent. All kinds of psychopathologies may result from this dynamic. It is impossible for us to deal with all this conditioning at the same time. A certain amount of focused inner work will be necessary to handle this mind-set, but an ongoing effort to be here now in love will automatically provide a defense.

Not all preoccupations are problematic. Whether they are or not hinges on the kind of internal questions or beliefs which are generating that particular preoccupation. When, for example, I am writing a book, there is a part of my mind that is always trying to present information in new and better ways. I have to keep an eye on this, of course, for I don't want it to become all-consuming. Yet, in spite of this sense of caution, the question, "How can I best express myself?" generates helpful, and even enjoyable thoughts. If I'm being here now in love, I will simply notice this as being a part of what's going on within and around me, and make some kind of decision about what to do with this information. Take note, we need to pay special attention to conditioning which may cause emotional pain and unpleasant thoughts. That is our concern.

FIGHT, FLIGHT, AND SEPARATION FROM HAPPINESS

What I am going to share in this section is a not-so-secret method for understanding most of your conditioning for unhappiness. *Simply observe* those times when you recoil from the present moment in an effort to control, manipulate, or hide from what's happening. This fight-or-flight response is a natural survival mechanism, inherent to our species' survival. When a threat is perceived, this mechanism is activated, preparing us physiologically for an immediate reaction: go to battle or escape the threat. Adrenaline levels rise, the heart rate increases, blood pressure elevates: we are on edge. You can see where this would be helpful if a saber-toothed tiger was standing at the mouth of your cave, but there are really very few such life-threatening situations in your daily life. The manner in which the human brain is "wired," however, makes it possible for us to generate the same fight-or-flight response as would the presence of a physical threat from a saber-toothed tiger.

Listed below are a few common triggers:

- you hear that the stock market has just fallen drastically
- your spouse becomes angry with you
- in the office, you see people talking with one another, and they keep looking at you
- you get caught in a traffic jam and know that you will be late for work
- the athletic team you root for is losing the game
- you notice that your hair is beginning to turn gray

The list could go on and on; we all have many "enemies" that promise to rob us of the conditions our minds have come to believe are necessary for happiness.

Every time the fight-or-flight mechanism kicks in, you are automatically separating yourself from the flow of life within and around you. The result is that you face the present moment with a guarded and controlling stance. Self-preservation becomes the most important concern. Countless times each day, down throughout the weeks, months, and years, this sense of self-separation is strengthened with the result that you come to feel isolated, lonely, and alienated from life itself. Your very identity appears to be rooted in this condition of being separated from life. Your self-image, desires, emotions, memories, everything that contributes to your ordinary sense of who you are, has now been colored by this conditioning. At this point, when you make decisions, you consult this new self-image which only serves to perpetuate this conditioning.

"What's wrong with this?" you ask. "Doesn't everybody live this way?"

What's wrong is that living as a result of this programming doesn't lead to lasting happiness. Oh, I'll grant you that there are times when the world "jumps through your hoops": people admire you, the money is coming in, your health is good, and other seemingly good things are happening. You come to have a sense of contentment about it all. But any and all of these can be taken away—*and you know it*! Lasting happiness cannot be attained by conditioning yourself to having things go your way. True happiness is without conditions, and, yes, there are very few people who are truly happy.

RELATING TO THE MOMENT

The ability to reverse your conditioning for unhappiness will happen, over time, as you continue to practice being here now in love. This is how it will happen.

While attempting to live in the present moment, something will happen either within you, or in the outside world, which triggers the fight-or-flight response. You notice that your attention is no longer in the now moment; you are caught up in a preoccupation of some kind (one of my friends calls this a "drama"). Stop and notice the theme of this preoccupation, and how it moves you to recoil from life, to become defensive and willful. Notice how your physical body is becoming tense, and feel what is happening. This awareness, in itself, is helpful to be able to let go of this separation-programming. Opening yourself to feeling this movement can help it become more diffused.

But you can do even more than this: *you can reclaim your power to choose a different response*, to reverse the contraction of your being, and to open yourself again to what is happening in the moment. This is an act of will made by a part of yourself that is not trapped in the old programming; this is the very thing that separates human beings from other animals (who act solely as a result of conditioning).

As a result, you can affirm new, loving beliefs about yourself:

- I am here now in God to love
- I will relate in love
- God is with me, loving now
- I can always handle what's happening in this moment

Reversing the contraction of your being away from life is the first movement of love in your soul. In his book *Will and Spirit: A Contemplative Psychology*, Dr. Gerald May, a psychiatrist working with the chemically dependent and a well-respected spiritual writer, calls this movement *willingness*. He considers it to be the essence of all spiritual practices. "Willingness," he writes, "implies a surrendering of one's self-separateness, an entering-into, an immersion in the deepest processes of life itself." One can also see a connection here with what the gospels calls *metanoia*, or a change of heart. I have found that it is impossible to maintain attentiveness to the present moment without this willingness. In its absence, the habitual dynamics of control and self-separation take over, spawning their never-ending currents of mental and emotional preoccupations. By practicing willingness, however, you become open to what is happening within and around you, as well as being attentive to what is required and able to receive what is offered. A prediction about what form this giving and receiving will take at any particular moment cannot always be clearly defined in advance. At times, especially when you are involved in what has been a difficult circumstance or relationship, it is good to have a plan that expresses willingness. Most of the time, however, it is far better to "enter into the dance," as many have called it, allowing willingness, attentiveness, and the marvelous intelligence which accompanies these qualities of spirit to guide your actions. The more you discover the joy and energy of living in this manner, the easier it will become to give up trying to control the moment.

PUTTING ATTENTIVE WILLINGNESS
INTO PRACTICE

Notice when your attention becomes distracted from life here and now and into a posture of self-preservation, control, or manipulation. Notice how this feels, note what happens to your breathing. If possible, try to identify the belief or expectation that has activated this fight-or-flight response.

In your prayer and meditation, be attentive to what you have discovered about your fight-or-flight mechanism and practice willingness affirmations when you do so.

Pray for guidance when you aren't sure about how willingness is leading you to respond to a situation. Remember that all of God's angels, saints, and the Spirit of God are at your disposal for such guidance. It is their pleasure to help you.

BREATH OF LIFE

As part of some of my workshops and retreats, I ask participants to stand and jump up and down. This physical activity serves to help circulate lymphatic fluids, and also wakes us all up! From the presenter's viewpoint, I can also say that it is rather funny to see your audience jumping up and down; it helps to take the edge off a little! How can you feel nervous when you find yourself in front of a group of adults who are jumping up and down and, eventually, laughing out loud about how ridiculous they all look?

After a minute or so of this jumping and laughing, some of the participants usually start to get winded. I call a halt to the activity and say, "OK, now I want you to take a d-e-e-e-p breath. Inhale deeply now, and hold it." (The reader is also invited to do the same at this time.) At this time, I ask them to notice the way they are holding their breath. "How many of you have sucked it all up into your upper chest and pulled your belly in?" Over 90 percent of them, on average, raise their hands. (Would you be a part of this group?) I instruct them, "Return to normal breathing now and have a seat, please."

DEFENSIVE BREATHING

If you have ever watched a dog or cat breathing while they sleep, you will note that their stomach area expands and contracts with each breath. It is the same with babies and small children. Sometimes, it is so pronounced, they seem to get a "big belly"! The reason behind this response is that they are drawing air into the upper and lower lobes of the lungs which pushes down on the stomach and intestines, causing the abdominal area to expand and bulge outward.

If this is the case with young children, why do adults breathe in just the opposite way? Most of us inhale air into the upper chest and exhale directly out from it, with very little movement in the abdomen. Why don't we use our abdomen to its fullest capacity?

The answer has to do with the fight-or-flight response we have discussed previously. When we feel threatened, the muscles in our abdominal area tighten. Breathing becomes more shallow and choppy, the result is that we draw less air into the lungs. If that happens repeatedly, there will be more permanent tension created in those muscles. This makes it difficult for the diaphragm to draw air into the lower lobes of the lungs. Our breath becomes more short and choppy as we accumulate feelings of anxiety and, in turn, repress them into the muscles of the body. To compensate, we try to draw more air into the upper lobes of the lungs, expanding our chest cavity as we inhale. This draws the diaphragm into the opposite direction of the natural movement we see in little children and animals. Breathing becomes reversed!

The consequences of this reversal are catastrophic! First, thoracic breathing (into the chest-upper lobes of the lungs) deprives the body of oxygen since we are filling only a small percentage of our lungs' capacity. With less oxygen, we have to take more breaths, the heart has to beat faster, and, as a result, the blood pressure rises. The body's tissues don't function at their full capacity without ample oxygen. Our physiology suffers.

The second consequence is that we lose touch with a mysterious center of life and intelligence located in the navel area. There are many nerves in this navel plexus; it is the place where we were once joined to our mothers in the womb. Long after we are born, we continue to have a special sensitivity to life in that area. This is the "gut center," where many of our intuitions and motives seem to be rooted. Small children and animals seem to breathe "into" and out of this center, as do enlightened people and mystics. They appear to be more "grounded," more alive in the present moment. I am convinced that their breathing pattern is a key to their sense of "aliveness." People who breathe into their upper chest area are out of touch with this "groundedness" and accompanying wisdom.

BREATH MEDITATION

If it is true that we breathe differently when we are stressed than when we are relaxed, what would happen if we were to breathe as though we were relaxed all of the time? What if we were to breathe as though we were little children, or even spiritually enlightened mystics? If our state of consciousness changes our breathing, then is it possible that changing our breathing can change our state of consciousness?

Indeed it is! This seems to be the premise behind many forms of meditation that emphasize attentiveness to breathing methods.

In 1987, I attended a Zen retreat. The form of meditation we were taught simply involved following our breathing and counting breaths. We were also taught to draw the breath "down" into the navel area and to exhale from there as well. Day after day, hour after hour, we sat doing this exercise which is called *zazen*. I found it to be very boring, so I joined my intention to love God and be loved by God to the breathing exercise and it helped. But let there be no question about it, my mind became quieter, my body more relaxed, and my attention centered in the here and now as a result. Even today, whenever my mind begins to become too unfocused, I return to this simple exercise. I find it quite effective.

Knowing that we breathe differently when we are in different emotional states has many practical applications. As mentioned earlier, our breathing is short and choppy when we are caught up in a fight-or-flight drama of some kind. By noticing your breathing, you can become more aware of this change. By changing your breathing, you can begin to move out of that state of anxiety. At the end of this section, I recommend a few simple breathing exercises to help you make this change.

Breathing is one of the few things we can do both consciously as well as unconsciously. When you want to change your breathing voluntarily, you can do so and when you don't, your breathing continues on its own. The act of becoming aware of your breathing awakens you to the existence of a place where the conscious and unconscious mind come together. Some forms of breath meditation (for example, those designed by Dr. Stanislov Grof, the creator of the breathing method called "Holotropic Breathing," and leading expert on non-ordinary states of consciousness) are designed to purge the unconscious of negative emotions and memories from the past. While this might seem extreme, it does illustrate some of the possibilities for using breath awareness as a means of healing. When we bring this dynamic into the spiritual life, we can invite God to work in both the conscious and unconscious aspects of the psyche.

An awareness of our manner of breathing is another excellent way to become more grounded of the present moment. There is a story about a disciple who asked Buddha how one could know if he was enlightened. His reply was, "To know that when you take a short breath that you are taking a short breath, and when you take a long breath that you are taking a long breath." The words "breath" and "spirit" have the same root (*ruah*), suggesting a connection between breathing and life. Living in close awareness of one's manner of breathing is a spiritual practice that can help us to become more attuned to the flow of life within us at each moment.

PUTTING BREATHING STRATEGIES INTO PRACTICE

Let breath awareness become part of your sensory checklist throughout the day. What is your breathing pattern? How does the air feel, how does it smell?

When you find that you are anxious, practice ten-by-ten breathing. Inhale deeply and hold for a slow count of ten; exhale everything and hold for a count of ten. Do this ten times, then let your breathing return to a new balance as you inhale the word *Shalom* (God's peace) and exhale whatever words express your stress. You will find that you have broken the fight-or-flight process, and, as a result, have an opportunity to choose another way to respond to your particular situation.

Another option may be to try some form of breath meditation. Begin this by noticing your breathing. Slowly, begin to inhale more deeply, inhale into the chest and heart, slowly draw your inhalation downward toward the navel area. Exhale from the navel up through the heart and chest. Notice the feel of your heart and navel area as you breathe. After a while, introduce a prayer word or phrase into your breathing. One ancient practice is to use the Jesus prayer: *Lord Jesus Christ* (while inhaling), *have mercy on me* (while exhaling). Let your own prayer words and phrases come to you, perhaps as an expression of your meditation on the Scriptures.

The following is an adaptation of the above exercise. In John 20:22–23, we read that Jesus breathed the Holy Spirit into his disciples, saying, "Receive the Holy Spirit. If you forgive the sins of any, they are forgiven them; if you retain the sins of any, they are retained." In your prayer, imagine that your inhalations are happening because Christ is exhaling them into you, and your exhalations are caused by his inhalations. Let Christ breathe into you, and allow your breath to adjust to whatever level and rhythm it seeks on its own, keeping your mind and will open to receiving the Holy Spirit.

TAKING RISKS

It takes courage to move from a life of self-protection to one of willingness, for this movement goes against the grain of much of our human conditioning. It is a fact that just about everyone you know loves and accepts you with certain "strings" attached. This leaves you always on the lookout for those special conditions by which you could be judged acceptable. Letting down your guard to become more open to the gift of the moment, to give and receive what is offered, implies you must become more vulnerable, and, therefore, more open to the possibility of being hurt. This is a risk that anyone who wants to be here now in love must take, however.

What is it that makes it possible for some people to take such a risk, to become more open to life through their sense of willingness, to let down their guard?

The answer to this is *courage*. The *American Heritage Dictionary* defines courage as "the state or quality of mind or spirit that enables one to face danger, fear, or vicissitudes with self-possession, confidence, and resolution; bravery." We can, then, conclude that those who have courage will be more willing to take the risk.

But there is another side to this: *those who take risks become people of courage*. Seldom does it seem that we have an over abundance of courage. We can truthfully say that the measure of the courage we need is the amount required to fortify us to take the risk that needs to be taken.

BECOMING COURAGEOUS

From my own personal experience, I have found that the key to being able to grow in courage has been to practice this virtue in small matters. Some circumstances will seem to present more risk than others. If I practice being lovingly attentive in situations where there is little risk of being hurt, I will, at least, have the opportunity to get in touch with the mechanics of opening myself to the moment so that, in other circumstances, where the risks are greater, I will know the way to courage.

One of the important lessons I've learned from this strategy is the fact that most of what I had considered risks were only risky with respect to my ego—accustomed as it was to fight-or-flight conditioning. For example, it seemed risky to share what I really felt with someone because he or she might not accept what I said. When I examined this closely, what I saw was that it was my fear of rejection that made this situation seem risky. That was my state of consciousness, but it was not one I wanted to maintain. Finding the courage to take the risk was aided by my desire to be free from this fear, which was making me miserable in so many ways. The freedom I experienced as a consequence of taking a risk provided further encouragement to take other, future risks.

I have since come to believe that *life is nothing but a constant flow of opportunities to be here now in love.* I mentioned this, previously, at the beginning of this book, but it needs to be stressed once again, here, in the context of taking risks. Loving attentiveness is the only way to live through stressful times without making things worse. *It is your attachment to having things turn out a certain way that is at the root of your anxiety*, for wherever there is such attachment, there is the fear that things might not happen as you would like. *When your strongest desire is to be here now in love, however, you can never be disappointed,* for you will always be able to fulfill this desire. You may have a preference about what you would like to see happen, but this should not be stronger than your willingness to accept the consequences of being here now in love. Nothing can deprive you of the joy of being here now in love, nothing except your own, fear-conditioned consciousness.

Whenever you find yourself in this situation, the temptation to collapse into the fight-or-flight mechanism is very strong. This means that such circumstances are the most ideal to practice attentiveness and willingness; if you can be here now in love when the going is rough, then you will be giving less energy and attention to your fearful self.

COURAGE IN ACTION

I once counseled a person who was experiencing frequent panic attacks. When these attacks came, she felt so terrible, that, at times, she even considered suicide. No medication or psychotherapy had been of any help, so she was meeting with me in the hope of finding a spiritual solution to her problem.

What soon became evident was that her fear of having another panic attack was almost as bad as the episodes themselves. Since she was a woman of faith, we talked about inviting God to be with her during these tough times, and simply accepting the attacks when they came, observing them without judgment, doing certain breathing exercises, such as those described previously, and just allowing it to pass. It was true, she acknowledged, they would always come and then pass, so would the next one as well. For 99 percent of the time, she was free from these panic attacks, and so why should she define her life in terms of the other 1 percent? By the time she left my office, she was almost eager for a panic episode to come so she could work through it as we had discussed! I gave her my phone number so she could call me if the going got too rough and she needed support, and set up an appointment for a month later.

She never called me, and, one month later, when she came for her appointment, she reported that she hadn't had any panic attacks at all since her last visit! "One started to come," she remarked, "but I called on the Spirit of God to be with me, brought my attention into the present moment, began breathing as you taught me, and prepared myself to welcome the energy and simply let it pass through. What happened next was amazing!" she exclaimed, with an exalted look on her face. "I started to feel that sick, sinking feeling, but instead of letting my mind resist and try to take control, I just observed it. I continued letting God breathe me into life, and within seconds, the fear went away and new energy began to diffuse throughout my whole body. I felt tingly from head to toe, and more enthusiastic to live my life than I can ever remember."

Ten years have passed since that exchange, and she has had other problems, but not a single panic attack. By facing her fear with courage and opening herself to its challenge, she overcame it. This may not be the ideal solution for everyone, but it is a step in the right direction. When you look at the entire picture, you can lose nothing and gain everything by this approach. You may even go so far as losing crippling anxiety and gaining more control of your life!

PUTTING RISK-TAKING INTO PRACTICE

From what kinds of risks do you tend to shy away? Make a list of them, and see how these avoidances rob you of your life.

Here is a *meditation exercise:* settle yourself into prayer, using some of the prayer methods I have previously described. Once you feel centered and open to God, consider one of the risky scenarios you put on your list. In your imagination, see yourself moving into this risky situation. Let yourself feel the anxiety, the tension, the onset of the fight-or-flight response, if it begins to happen. Ask God to breathe courage into your spirit, and be aware of your own breathing as you continue to consider this risky situation. See yourself responding in faith, courage, and love. Feel the strength building in your heart and abdominal region. Continue breathing in the Spirit until you feel you have faced this situation satisfactorily. Know that you will always respond in this way in a similar situation.

In the future, whenever you are faced with a risky situation, notice how you are responding. Be aware of the sensations, and make note of the risk to yourself and to God. Let your breathing become slower and deeper as you call on the Spirit to help you be here now in love. Ask for guidance to respond lovingly. Repeat the phrase, "I can do all things in Christ, who strengthens me."

LIVING IN FAITH

There was once a time in my own life when I was struggling with depression. I had little self-confidence, and little courage to do anything to change. A friend gave me a book entitled *Man's Search for Meaning* by Viktor Frankl. In it, I read about his experiences in Nazi concentration camps, and his discovery that those prisoners who could maintain a sense of meaning actually lived longer than those who couldn't. In most cases, it was their religious faith that gave them a sense of meaning; for some, faith in God was to such an extent that they were able to be generous and patient with others in spite of their cruel environment.

I thought to myself that my own situation was certainly no worse than theirs had been. I had plenty of food, water, and opportunities for relationships and a good job. If a sense of meaning in life was able to help them so much, then why wasn't it helping me? Any one of those prisoners would have happily traded circumstances with me, yet I was incapable of showing just a small fraction of their virtue and gratitude. I had religious faith, as they did, but I just needed to learn to put it into practice.

What followed was a couple of years of working diligently on my attitude. I went on retreats, wrote journals about my feelings, prayed, meditated, attended workshops, and met with a spiritual director—and it all helped! God's grace, working through my efforts, helped me become less negative and more courageous, more grateful and less depressed. My attention began to rest more and more spontaneously in the present moment; life became enjoyable.

FAITH AND JUDGMENTALISM

One of the most important lessons I learned as a result of my bout with depression is that one's emotional states are closely related to the judgmental thoughts we have in a certain situation. These judgmental thoughts, in turn, are related to our beliefs. If I am depressed and believe that people don't like me, or that I'm ugly, or without any value, my own depression will only deepen. If, on the other hand, I begin to counter those beliefs with positive ones that are true, I quit reinforcing the emotion and immediately begin to feel better.

But how does one change a set of beliefs? What beliefs are wholesome, true, and meaningful? Upon which convictions will I build my life? These were the kinds of questions upon which I reflected. I searched among various learned theories of philosophy and psychology for answers, but, in the end, was led deeper into my own religious faith, where I found the answers I was seeking and the beliefs that brought me healing and hope.

What do I mean by faith? Once again, the *American Heritage Dictionary* brings some clarity. Faith is

1. Confident belief in the truth, value, or trustworthiness of a person, an idea, or a thing.

2. Belief that does not rest on logical proof or material evidence.

3. Loyalty to a person or thing; allegiance.

4. Often Faith. Theology. The theological virtue defined as secure belief in God and a trusting acceptance of God's will.

5. The body of dogma of a religion.

6. A set of principles or beliefs.

By using the word "faith," I mean all of the above, especially if these beliefs engender in a person a sense of the trustworthiness of God and life. Trust is at the heart of willingness and courage, and belief can certainly move a person to trust.

Trust implies opening yourself to the unknown, to mystery, to possibilities you have not yet explored.

Since every moment is unique and pregnant with mystery, it takes trust to open yourself to the gift of the moment.

Belief is a two-edged sword, however, so a person must be careful with respect to what kinds of beliefs he or she has. Beliefs are thought patterns which have been committed to memory. Many beliefs may be harmful. The fear-driven ego, for example, is informed by a whole array of beliefs about how one should be and what one should do in order to be successful, acceptable, in control, and so forth. Such beliefs do not encourage trust, however, and eventually need to become uprooted and drained of energy. This can be done once they are seen for what they are, and making the choice to trust yourself in the flow of life now, instead of choosing to follow their dictates.

In many ways, the whole body of Scripture, especially the Resurrection of Jesus, is a testament to the goodness of life and the trustworthiness of God—a coming together of religion and spirituality in a mutually beneficial way. Religious teachings that help to promote trust, risk-taking, willingness, and attentiveness are very good. So is liturgy, when it supports these disciplines. Religious beliefs provide the intellect with food to support the awareness and will in the practice of being here now in love. The intellect is part of our human nature, and even though much of its functions have become co-opted by the fearful ego, its contribution to living a spiritual life is not to be denied. Theology, doctrine, Scripture, and spiritual reading all help to transform the intellect and its understanding of God, human nature, creation, and the meaning of life.

The following is a sampling of scriptural passages that can help to support trust:

1. "God is love, and those who abide in love abide in God, and God abides in them" (1 Jn 4:16).

2. We know that all things work together for good for those who love God..." (Rom 8:28).

3. "The one who is in you is greater than the one who is in the world" (1 Jn 4:4).

When you act on such convictions as expressed above, you draw the very presence and energy of God into your actions, so that your practice of attentiveness and willingness becomes a means by which God blesses other people and all of creation through you. In doing so, you are blessed as well, for the process of blessing confers blessedness on both the giver and receiver. A wonderful life becomes available to those whose faith leads them to be here now in love.

"You are the light of the world. A city built on a hill cannot be hid. No one after lighting a lamp puts it under the bushel basket, but on the lampstand, and it gives light to all in the house. In the same way, let your light shine before others, so that they may see your good works and give glory to your Father in heaven" (Mt 5:14–16). They become like these lights, while the rest of the world hides the light under bushel baskets of fearful defenses. This light attests to the truth of our faith more surely than any course in theological apologetics could ever accomplish. Faith, then, leads to experiential knowledge of God (knowledge based on experience), which is the saving grace of our lives.

PUTTING FAITH INTO PRACTICE

What kinds of beliefs keep you from taking risks? (Hint: examine your response to the statement, is it something along the lines of, "I'll be OK when…"?)

Make a list of faith-affirmations which can move you to exercise trust and courage.

Imagine God speaking about these to you, picture him telling you the following:

1. You are my child. I love you very much.

2. I have a mission for you. I need you to fulfill it.

3. I am with you wherever you go and in whatever you do.

4. I will give you what you need to accomplish what has to be done.

5. You have been created in my image and likeness.

Add your own thoughts to this list.

DISCERNING

Recently, my wife was late coming home from work. This has happened many times without causing me much anxiety, but what was unique to this particular situation was that the weather had become very cold and icy. Other times in the past she almost always called when she was running late, but there was no call this time. A half-hour passed, then an hour, and I was becoming very worried. I called her place of employment, and they confirmed that she had left. That's all I knew.

At some point during my anxious moments, however, I woke up to what was really happening. This was a situation that was beyond my control, and I was activating the fight-or-flight response with increasing intensity because all the negative "what if..." scenarios I was creating in my mind. I reflected upon what I could do to help in this situation, and discovered that I could exert no practical influence whatsoever, other than to pray for her safety. I did so, then switched to being here now in love—or tried to, at least! The negative thinking and feeling that I had set into motion continued to cloud my awareness, but I chose not to indulge them any longer. The worry began to diminish, and, within minutes I was back to the flow of life, mysteriously consoled, somehow, that my wife was safe. A short while later, while I was working in the kitchen, I happened to look at the calendar and noticed that she had a meeting to go to after work, and would be home later than usual. All of my worrying had been based on the premise that was never valid in the first place: that she was late! She eventually did come home safely after her meeting.

THOUGHTS, ENERGY, AND THE LIGHT

This episode, and many like it, have deeply impressed upon me the relationship that exists between thoughts and energy. I have learned that the energy of life, when untainted by negative desires, is sweet, intelligent, nurturing, and blissful. When people experience life in such a pure manner, their faith comes alive, and the presence of God as the Intelligence behind the flow of life is immediately known through their intuition. Both complete self-forgetfulness and, paradoxically, complete self-awareness are at work during such times. This awareness of self and God are not, in any way separate, and are, by no means, a product of intellectual reflection. This kind of experience is what has been called the *True Self*. It is the heritage of every human being.

You might compare the True Self experience to white light. White light, as physicists have learned, contains all the colors of the spectrum that are known to humankind. When you hold a prism before a white light, it separates these colors, giving us the effect of a rainbow. Each color is not separate from the white light, but part of it, existing at a particular wave length within that light.

It is the same with God and all of creation. *The Light of God* contains all things, yet all things are each unique expressions and manifestations of that Light. These creatures, animate and inanimate, possess different capacities for intelligence and freedom for manifesting the Light: capacities which belong to the creature that may be used to manifest or restrict the appearance of the Light. Therefore, what is manifest in all creatures is naught but the one Light that is refracted by the form being given to the creature by its Creator, and by the form the creature has given itself because of its own conditioning. To establish contact with anything in creation is to make contact with both the creature and God who is being manifest through the creature. This is an experiential truth for those whose hearts and minds have been purified.

Human beings have been given a very mighty power: the ability to form reality through the use of thought. Thought, as such, is the capacity to form and shape energy. It is a sharing in the Word, or form-giving activity in God. Every thought within us, either conscious or not, is, therefore, giving some form to our energy. When the mind is at peace and the will is open and loving, the Light shines freely, and the energy which moves through us is Love itself. Because we are connected with one another and to all of creation in God, we bring the Light of God more fully into the universe.

LEARNING THE ART OF DISCERNMENT

Living a spiritual life makes it necessary for you to, ultimately, take responsibility for the thoughts that are happening in your field of consciousness. All of the thoughts that happen inside of you are shaping both your life as well as creation. Each and every one of them! Many have come into your psyche from other people (here, I also include the culture in which one lives), who communicated them to you in such a way that they have become "stuck" inside you as beliefs. Some of these are for the better, but many are not. Knowing the ultimate origin of these thoughts is sometimes helpful, but not always necessary. But it is absolutely essential for you to recognize what thoughts you're consenting to, for, in so doing, you give more energy to the thought. That enables it to shape you more deeply according to its particular dynamism. If you consent to thoughts such as "I'm a failure," you reinforce that dynamic in your being, and then create a self-fulfilling prophecy. If you think you're a failure, you feel like one, your body gets this message, and you eventually act like one, bringing this thought to its full manifestation. You might not have placed this thought in your mind to begin with, but your ongoing consent to it is the aspect you can change.

Thoughts which enable you to entrust yourself to the gift of life at each moment are, obviously, very worthy of your consent. Thoughts which move you to contract your will and attention from the moment, thus activating the fight-or-flight response, are to be rejected. *Discernment is the practice of becoming aware of these two polarities present in thoughts, and choosing the one to which you will give your consent.*

Consent, here, refers to an act of will, which is, in turn, ultimately influenced by thoughts, beliefs, and experiences. It means choosing to allow one course of action over another. Not allowing or consenting doesn't mean repressing, but simply not attending to it. When you repress something, you are attending to it, relating to it, and giving energy to it, all the while hoping that it won't become manifest (which it cannot help but eventually do simply because you are attending and energizing it). When you switch your energy away from a certain line of thought, however, neither repressing nor expressing it, but just ignoring it, you remove from it the energy to manifest. Without energy, a thought can do nothing, and, as a result, it eventually dissipates or languishes like a sailboat in a calm ocean, awaiting the next time the winds of energy will blow it again to its formative destination.

You cannot take responsibility for the totality of all your thoughts at once, of course. Some thoughts are deep down, working very subtly in the unconscious as a result of certain long-held beliefs: you may not even be aware of them! Others come to mind here and now and these are the thoughts you can change.

What you must do is simply persevere in a willingness to be here now in love. When thoughts come along and take over, you observe what has happened, what these thoughts are about, and what responses they set in motion. If they activate the fight-or-flight response, or move you into preoccupations so that you're out of touch with the moment, you can recognize this, acknowledge it, and simply say, "Oh, I've gotten caught up in it." You then say a short prayer for whatever your concern has been, asking God to care for it now (called "turning it over" in Twelve Step groups), and then move on. Just withdraw your attention from those lines of thought. *Drop them!* They will linger for a while, like heat in a burner that has just lost its fire, but eventually they will cool. Then, at that time, the next level of distraction and preoccupation will come, and you will deal with it in the same manner. That's what discernment it all about, and it goes on all day, every day.

Perhaps you will have thought patterns that you just can't move away from in the same way as described above. At times, people have had negative thoughts drilled into them for so long that these patterns seem to have a life of their own. When you discover one of these, whether it's an addiction, or an attachment to approval, or a source of shame, you might need to seek professional help, or undertake very focused, formal exercises in order to uproot these negative thoughts from your psyche. A simple rule of thumb is *if you can't do it on your own, get some help.* You would seek professional help (a dentist) if you had a toothache that wouldn't go away, so do the same with emotional aches that just don't go away. The therapeutic process and the formal exercises you undertake will be most helpful if they focus on understanding what this pattern is, how it operates, what consequences it brings, how you give your consent to it, and the tools to show you how you can withdraw your consent. This may cause a painful reliving of certain traumatic events, if they are the cause. This cannot be predicted, but the benefits gained certainly are worth the risk.

FINDING FREEDOM IN TRUTH

I used to think that goodness, love, and happiness were values I had to create through my own efforts. Once, I even thought that religion could help me know what these "right efforts" were. What I have come to realize, from the practice of being here now in love, is that life, love, and happiness are gifts given to us at each moment, and there is nothing we can personally do to create them. This circumstance is true because God is creating, in each moment, what is already good, loving, and happy. When we awaken at the level of the True Self, we know the goodness of God's creation to be true. When, however, we are consenting to live in negative, constricting thoughts, we lose this awareness, and begin trying to create something which approximates it through our own efforts. Sometimes, we may succeed momentarily, but whatever we create can be lost, and, as a result, our experiences of happiness are conditional, and ultimately bracketed by the fear of loss and death.

Contemplate the following statements:

1. In order to know happiness, you need only to drop your unhappiness, and there it is, blessing you.

2. To know love, you need only drop your non-love, and there it is, loving you.

3. To know life, you need only drop death, and there you are, alive.

4. To know the True Self, you need only be here now in love.

This is the message that true religion communicates. It is the message of Christ.

PUTTING DISCERNMENT INTO PRACTICE

Be aware, throughout the day, of the thoughts you are having, and the directions where your thoughts want to lead you. Be especially sensitive to the movements of personal willfulness and willingness to change.

Practice the following *Consciousness Exam*:

At the end of the day, prayerfully review your day and its events. *When did you feel close to God? When did you stray from God, going off in your own direction? What were you feeling? What unfinished business did you have? What concerns still required your prayers? What unhealthy beliefs forced you to act?* You can do this in an informal way, keying in on only one or two of these questions.

Part Two

Practices That Promote Freedom to Live in the Here and Now

hat do you do when you're sad, angry, lonely, fearful? These are times when it's very difficult to be lovingly aware, for the focus is on "me" and "my problems." The more intense the feeling, the more self-focused we become. This response is only natural. However, there are healthy responses to each of those experiences, but most of us also learned the unhealthy ones. In fact, some people learned almost *exclusively* the unhealthy habits, and have paid the price because of it.

FASTING FROM QUICK FIXES

The most common of these unhealthy responses is the *quick fix*, defined here as *the use of any substance or activity to change one's mood without resolving the emotional predicament at its root*. There are healthy ways to change one's mood, but these involve feeling emotions and working with them. The object of a quick fix, however, is to prevent you from feeling your emotions, making it impossible to learn what they are trying to communicate to you.

Almost anything can function as a quick fix. Alcohol and drugs are the quick fixes par excellence because they directly change the chemistry of nerve impulse transmissions. When you use them, you feel better for a short while, or, at least, you don't feel what you were previously feeling. Junk food does almost the same thing and is a much more common quick fix. Activities like watching television, gambling, work, sex, shopping, surfing the Internet, and reading can be means of escape, as can relationships, and even religious activities. *It's not the substance or activity, per se, that constitutes the quick fix, but how it is used.* When we use something to avoid experiencing our emotions, we are indulging in a quick fix of some kind.

One of my several past career choices was as a drug and alcohol-abuse counselor. While in training for this profession, I, as well as other potential counselors, were asked to examine our lives to see what addictions we were using to "escape from ourselves." I was neither an alcoholic, drug addict, gambling addict, nor a sex addict, or any such thing, but I could surely identify with people who were, and particularly with some of their attitudes. I, too, had difficulty experiencing my emotions, and even more trouble expressing them appropriately. Although I wasn't in "over my head" with any particular fix, what I learned was that I also used a multitude of fixes all day long to keep myself out of touch with emotional pain. I drank coffee, smoked cigarettes, ate junk food, read trashy novels, watched TV sports, listened to the current popular tunes on the radio. I did none of these to great excess, mind you, but all in sufficient quantity and frequency to keep me out of touch with my feelings. I recognized this and called myself a multiple "fix-aholic."

The more I shared my story with others, the more I learned that we were the same. We're probably all multiple fix-aholics, but for some, one of the fixes becomes predominant and problematic in its own right. For example, excessive alcohol drinking causes health and relationship problems, gambling depletes finances, overeating binges bring on weight gain or even purging, just to name a few. In such cases, the addictive fix of choice has become a "primary problem" because it must be dealt with before any real growth can happen.

Our use of fixes is a consequence of our human brokenness. Most of us were all raised in an environment of conditional love; we were all loved *because*. This love "with strings attached" has left us feeling only conditionally lovable, acceptable, and capable with accompanying anxiety, shame, sadness, resentment, and loneliness. To make matters worse, many of us learned that it was not acceptable to express these emotions, for when we did, there was only more discounting of our feelings, or their outright rejection. So, as a result, we found fixes, ways to numb our emotions so that we could continue to live without feeling too badly! In addition, we developed a wide range of defenses to keep other people away from these feelings. This makes sense: what else were we supposed to do? Total emotional vulnerability and authenticity are not really options in this fallen world, not unless you're with someone you can really, really trust. Like God!

FIXES AND SPIRITUALITY

As we grow in our relationship with God, we will find that our fixes and inner defenses are obstacles to belonging to God. God loves us even with all these problems, but that is not the issue. The issue is that, just as our fixes and defenses kept us from being vulnerable to other people, they keep us from opening up to God as well. They also prevent us from being honest and present before God, from being able to say, "Here I am!" just as Moses did before the burning bush. When I turn on the TV to avoid feeling my loneliness, I am running away from myself, and from God. In fact, I am using the TV as a god of sorts, as a higher power upon which I can focus my life in order to achieve happiness and healing. Fixes are, therefore, false idols of sorts, so you can see why they're a problem in the spiritual life.

What are we to do? Do we just get rid of all our fixes? Then what?

No, you can't get rid of all your fixes right away. But you can begin to know when you're using them. In your ongoing effort to be here now in love, you can become more aware of your inner states, and of what you're doing to deal with them.

You can practice self-honesty, saying to yourself such things as *I really do want chocolate candy now! What's the feeling hidden behind this desire? What do I really want?*

This kind of honesty and reflection will bring you to a place more in touch with your deeper experiences, and liberate more energy in your soul.

You can also begin to identify which fixes seem the most destructive and predominant in your life. In my case, it was cigarettes. I gave them up, suffered withdrawals, felt my crankiness, relapsed, and gave them up again, finally arriving at the place where I am now, completely free from them (this took years, by the way). Next, I cut down on my use of the TV and radio, consulting them only when I was genuinely interested. I also went from drinking seven cups of coffee a day to three.

With the removal of each fix, my inner life, including its accompanying negative energies, became more available to me. I had to learn to live with these (we'll speak more about this later on). However, I could not deny the fact that, even with these unpleasant emotions, I felt more alive and alert than ever. I also felt God's presence more strongly in my life.

PURGING QUICK FIXES IN PRACTICE

Ask yourself these questions:

- What fixes do I use in my life to avoid unpleasant emotions?
- What fix(es) are predominant? What kinds of consequences do I suffer because of them? Consider the physical, mental, emotional, spiritual, moral, financial, social, and legal aspects.

Taking the above into consideration:

- Resolve to drop at least one fix this week.
- Become more aware of when you are using fixes. Ask yourself what emotion or desire is it that you are trying to escape? Let yourself experience this emotion or desire without the fix.

DROPPING YOUR HARMFUL ATTACHMENTS

One of the most liberating lessons I have learned is that I don't really have to do anything to make myself acceptable. It's not that I'm the perfect weight, or have financial security, or anything like that. These are all ongoing struggles. But I don't have to postpone happiness, or my enjoyment of life, until these conditions are met. I can "be OK," even in the midst of the "mess." There are many times when I experience this acceptance, not only intellectually, but within my whole being, so I know it's not just a "good idea." There's a profound truth here, one that we can all experience.

Mark Twain once said, "I'm an old man now, and in my life, I've known lots of problems, most of which were not real." There *are* real problems in the world, to be sure. But there are many more unreal ones!

What the wise, old humorist was referring to is all the ways we make ourselves miserable because of our attitudes and conditioning. Growing up, as we all have, in a fallen world, characterized by conditional love and acceptance, we received the message early on that we had to *do something* to become lovable and acceptable. In and of ourselves, we were not-OK, or not-totally-OK. Maybe we were almost OK, but this is still a far cry from the unconditional love and acceptance that should have been our birthright. Instead, we experienced anxiety and feelings of inner inadequacy, even shame, which prompted our minds to work to find ways to resolve this inner dilemma.

THE WAYS OF WORLDLY ATTACHMENTS

One of our solutions, as we have already noted, is to develop defenses and use fixes. These strategies helped to take the edge off our pain. Yet another response was to embark on the life-long task of *making ourselves OK.*

How would we do this? We may try many various methods but they fall short of the mark. They fail because of what they all have in common, they are strategies which belong to what Scripture calls "the World." The World, as an enemy of God, does not mean the created Earth, for this, Scripture tells us, is very good. The World refers to all those cultural traditions which we adopt in an effort to correct our inner disharmony by making ourselves OK. Physical beauty, social status, material wealth, power, control, popularity, these values are held out by the World as ways to happiness. If we get too frustrated in pursuit of them, we can turn to our fixes. The result is that we eventually become attached, even addicted, to these values.

But why do none of these strategies work? Oh, they might deliver a temporary thrill, or we might be "successful" in one or more of these pursuits, every now and then. But they do not resolve our inner brokenness, and they do not satisfy the heart. Furthermore, anything we attain through worldly pursuits can be taken away, so there is always an ingrained anxiety in the background. We see people and circumstances in terms of whether they are either a help or a hindrance to our worldly pursuits. Those which threaten this fulfillment activate the fight-or-flight response, which we discussed previously (page 30) about willingness. It is impossible to be here now in love when your mind has been polluted by the world.

THE QUEST FOR OK-NESS
AND WORLDLY ATTACHMENTS

There is really nothing wrong with pursuing physical beauty, wealth, power, status, or anything which does not hurt others. In terms of the spiritual life, what makes these pursuits worldly is that we define our happiness in terms of their fulfillment. We can't be OK unless.... This is the attitude at the root of all attachments.

It was quite a revelation to me to discover this. I had been working on letting go of fixes and attachments, focusing on the behaviors themselves, rather than the underlying attitudes. What I discovered was that no sooner had I given up one attachment (to popularity and recognition, for example), than another crept in to take its place. *Why*, I wondered, *do I keep doing this to myself?*

I discovered that underneath all my specific attachments was a belief that I was only conditionally lovable and acceptable. This left me feeling anxious and flawed, prompting my mind to "fix myself" through my attachments. The "I'll-be-OK-when" mental virus was stuck in my soul, and it was utilizing considerable intellectual, emotional, and volitional resources. I was forever on the lookout for ways to make myself OK, strategies that the World offers in abundance. Even my religious involvements were, in part, attempts to make myself OK by doing the kinds of things that would please God and get God's approval.

What I needed to do was give up this attitude of "I'll be OK when..." and accept that my inner anxiety and shame would never be healed by *doing things*. Only by allowing God's unconditional love to touch those deep-down parts of me could I be healed.

It was amazing to see just how much I resisted this healing. I knew God's love was real, and that I needed healing, but the pursuit of attachments had given me a sense of being in control of my happiness, of being able to *do something* to make myself OK. To give this up meant to rely upon something or someone else, to relinquish control. Trying as hard as I was able, I could not completely give up control. All I could do was express to God my willingness to give up control; the rest was up to grace. And grace is given! The attachment to being in control through "I'll be OK when" is weakened each day. It is a process of consciously letting go and inviting God *to be God* for me. It seems that God requires this kind of permission-giving, he will not barge in and take over.

I can always tell now when this "I'll-be-OK-when" attitude begins to be activated, for I begin to feel disturbed and upset. I have come to see that it's not the problems of life themselves that disturb me, for we will always have problems to some degree. What disturbs me is the "I'll-be-OK-when-this-problem-is-resolved" attitude! Just to notice and give this particular dynamic a name is the beginning of liberation. To work to drop it by countering its false promises is the next step.

Some days, I spend a great deal of time telling myself, *No, it's really OK to be here now with this problem, to live with it, and love with it. God is here, now, loving you and everything in this context. Wake up!* If I do this and don't cooperate with the attachment, it will come to pass, and, lo and behold, I discover that happiness has been there all along!

When we stop making ourselves miserable through attachments, we wake up to our inherent goodness, peace, and happiness. How simple! How difficult to realize!

PUTTING DETACHMENT INTO PRACTICE

What are some of your attachments and subsequent strategies for trying to make yourself OK?

Consider the following: getting approval, recognition, impressing others, material wealth, social status, physical beauty, power, and control. (Remember, inner disturbance is almost always a sign that an attachment of some kind has been activated.)

Now, pick out one attachment and see how much it influences your decisions. See the kinds of emotions you experience because of it, the highs, the lows, the inner preoccupations. Write these down in a journal.

Try to envision yourself living without this attachment. Picture yourself in a situation where it is usually triggered, but now you choose a different way, one that's about loving, to respond. *Let yourself truly feel what it would be like to act in a different manner in this situation.*

Speak directly to your distorted beliefs at the root of this attitude. Name them, expose their faulty logic, call upon the Spirit to help you articulate a healthy alternative affirmation.

Follow these steps for any other attachments you recognize in your daily life.

NONJUDGMENTAL THINKING

All of the world's great mystical traditions teach that non-judgmental awareness is essential to a contemplative experience. They speak of "just-looking," of accepting things as they are, of not condemning others, and so forth.

But what does that mean? Does it mean that one cannot

pronounce moral judgment about a situation, or that one has no opinions about anything?

No. Nonjudgmental awareness does not mean that a person has no moral values, nor does it mean they avoid pronouncing moral judgment when this is needed. We see, from the life of Jesus, that he confronts evil, takes moral stands, and works for justice. But, at the same time, he also tells us, "Do not judge, so that you may not be judged. For with the judgment you make you will be judged, and the measure you give will be the measure you get" (Mt 7:1–2). He goes one to say, "Why do you see the speck in your neighbor's eye, but do not notice the log in your own eye?" (Mt 7:3).

Judging has to do with the preconceptions we have about other people, and even of the circumstances in which we find ourselves. This kind of judging has a profound effect on our relationships and our openness to life.

In the Book of Genesis, we read that the serpent tempted Adam and Eve to eat of the fruit by telling them, "God knows that when you eat of it your eyes will be opened, and you will be like God, knowing good and evil" (3:5). It has been this same way ever since: human beings walking about the planet saying, "this is good and that is bad," acting like gods themselves. To be sure, there *is* right and wrong, good and evil, truth and falsehood. But much of what we spend our time judging as good and bad is neither, except in respect to our own personal preferences and preconceptions.

The following are some common examples of how we misuse our power to pass judgments:

1. *About other people.* We judge them to be good and bad, and this is just plainly wrong. We do not know the inner life, or heart, of another. We are free to judge their ac-

tions, but not their motives, and certainly not their person-hood.

2. *About our health.* We say it is good when we feel well and bad when we're sick. Actually, it is neither good nor bad: it just is! There are either pleasant or unpleasant consequences which come with health, but this is neither good nor bad. Many times, we learn more about ourselves and God when we are sick than when we are healthy.

3. *About the weather.* Obviously, the weather has no moral will capable of manifesting good and evil. Weather is only good or bad with respect to our needs and desires. When it rains, the farmer often cheers, while the vacationer groans. Neither should pass judgment, however. Weather just is.

4. *About circumstances.* These just exist, except, of course, with reference to our desires and preferences. (More about this shortly.)

When we pass judgment, we affect the way we relate to a situation. By saying that something or someone is bad, we close ourselves to the reality, we may even harden ourselves to it. This produces consequences within us that affect the way we view everything else. This is why Jesus said, "Do not judge, so that you may not be judged." When we judge, we are judged by the dynamism set in motion by the very act of judging.

ATTACHMENTS AND PASSING JUDGMENT

As I have mentioned previously, I worked as an alcohol and drug counselor in a psychiatric hospital (from 1985 to 1990). One of the lessons most deeply impressed upon me was how certain situations, for the addicts, gradually become viewed in terms of how that helped or hindered their addiction. People and circumstances which helped them to "use" were judged as being good; those which frustrated their usage were judged as being bad; those which neither helped nor threatened were hardly even noticed.

This prompted me to take a look at my own life. I saw how I did exactly the same thing! I was constantly evaluating things with reference to what I wanted or did not want, and hardly noticed what fell outside of this frame of reference. I was just like those addicts, perhaps not quite so rigid...yet!

Judging people and circumstances in terms of how they help or hinder the fulfillment of our attachments is surely the most destructive of all kinds of judgments, yet we do it on a variety of levels. To give you a current example, it seems that every time the OPEC nations raise the price of oil, our attitude toward people native to that country becomes pretty nasty. This threatens our national attachment to cheap gasoline and all that this makes possible. Ask yourself this: *How often do I judge those of other Christian denominations, or even people of other religions, because they threaten my own belief that I am "right" in such matters?* Attachments, in other words, are not simply a personal affair; social and national attachments exist as well. These provoke judgments and defensive behavior when a certain "wish" fulfillment is threatened.

THE TRAP OF PRECONCEPTIONS

Several years ago, I read about a study involving teachers and expectations. None of the teachers knew they were part of a research project, but all were informed, in advance, that they would be teaching one of three classes of students: one group that was very bright and gifted, or another that was an ordinary blend of students, or a group of learning-impaired students. In reality, all the classes included in the study were the usual blend of quick-thinkers and slow-learners, so what was really being evaluated in the research was how the teachers' expectations affected learning outcomes at the end of the year.

The results were sobering; *there was a direct correlation between teacher expectation and student outcome.* The teachers who thought they were teaching bright students had students who scored better on tests than did those who thought they had an "ordinary class." The most negative outcome happened in classes where the teachers had been told that the group was "slow." Although it would be risky to draw too many moral or spiritual conclusions from this study, it does demonstrate rather well the formative power of human judgment.

The teachers had preconceptions about their students, they had fixed ideas about who they were, and how they would act. We all do the exact same thing. We interact with someone or some situation for a short while, and formulate a concept, or image, of what that person, or situation, is like. It is natural for the mind to do this; it's what makes knowledge, and even language, possible. Yet there is a problem with this: we begin to see things "through" the lenses of the concept, projecting "how we think things are." In such cases, *we don't see things as they truly are, but as we are, and this is an illusion.* When the object of our perception begins to deviate significantly from our preconception about how we think it should be or act, we frequently judge it negatively and try to get it to "shape up" so it will behave according to our preconceptions.

A good example of this is at family reunions. You haven't seen many of these people for a good, long time, and you have grown and changed in many ways since the time when you were once close to them. As you make contact once again, you discover that they relate to you as you once were, as though you haven't changed at all over the years. They are relating to you through their memory of you, which is not the real you, only their idea of who you are. If they can't stop this pattern and begin to expand their understanding, you will find yourself frustrated, or even drawn to act as though you were the person they imagine you to be. Like the students in the previous example, you will either feel moved to meet the expectations set up for you, or you will rebel and reject them.

Preconceptions can also apply to yourself. You have a certain self-concept, and you're always comparing who you are and what you do with this idea. You can't help doing this, for your mind doesn't know how else to comprehend who you are. But what you can know is that *you are more than your self-concept*, and you need not judge yourself on the basis of that self-concept. If you think you are fat, ugly, stupid, or the like, that's only because you're making a comparison between your self-concept and other people who, you believe, "have done it right." Stop comparing yourself to them, just accept who you are without passing judgment. You can be as happy as a lark even if you think you fall short of the mark!

Finally, we also have preconceptions about who God is, and how God acts. We've formed a God-concept based upon what we've been taught about God, and what we've experienced for ourselves. We relate to God from within this concept, and project God's probable responses in terms of it.

Even if your God-concept is very theologically updated, however, the problem is that God is so much more than our conception of him ever could be! The Church has solemnly taught us that any idea we have about God is just as incorrect as it is correct. For example, we say that God is love, and indeed God is! But what does love mean? Does it mean what people do to show favor to one another? If your father was mean to you, does it help to say that God is our Father? These kinds of ideas tell us something about God that moves our attention toward God, but if we want to know the real God, we have to move beyond the idea to the Mystery. It is the same for your encounters with others, yourself, and all of creation.

PUTTING NONJUDGMENTALISM INTO PRACTICE

To become less judgmental consider the following recommendations:

1. *Try to be aware of times when you're judging people and circumstances.* See how your attachments spawn judgments by noticing the thoughts going on in your mind when you feel disturbed about something.

2. *What kinds of ideas about yourself cause you to judge yourself so harshly?* Write these down in your journal, and for each of them, repeat the following: "I am neither good nor bad because of you. I am who I am, and that is good enough for God."

3. *What kinds of ideas about God prevent you from opening yourself to God?* Write these down as well. For each of these, say: "God is more wonderful than this idea I have. Help me to know the real You, dear God."

4. *Practice acceptance.* Avoid saying things like "the weather is good," make no judgments. Just let things be as they are, and see how they present opportunities to give and receive Love.

LET GO OF THE PAST

There is a wonderful story about two monks on a journey to visit a distant monastery. Along the way, they came upon a wide and deep river, which could only be crossed by wading across part of the way and then swimming the rest. A beautiful young woman was waiting on the bank. She begged them to help her across the river, stating she could not swim. The younger monk, remembering his vow of celibacy and personal resolve to avoid sexual impurity, ignored her request and started to cross the river. The older monk, however, invited her to climb on his back and cross the water with him. She grasped him tightly, and they, too, entered the river and made their way across. Once on the other shore, the woman climbed off the monk's back, thanked him profusely, and went on her way.

The two monks continued on their journey, walking along for a few miles in silence. Finally, the young monk exploded: "I can't believe you allowed that beautiful young woman to climb on your back to cross the river! What about your vow of celibacy; your purity of thought? What would other people say if they knew what had happened?" He continued in this manner for a few minutes longer, castigating the older monk for his good deed.

The old monk listened patiently, and when the younger one was finished, he said: "Brother, I dropped that young woman off once I reached the bank of that river. Why are you still carrying her?"

Many of us are like that young monk. We carry around our emotions from the past, and these prevent us from being here now in love. Indeed, we might go so far as to say that *whenever we experience emotions from the past, we are in the past.* You may ask:

What's wrong with that? Aren't we supposed to remember the past? Living in the past is not the same as remembering it. The problem with living in the past is that life is happening here and now, so when we live in the past, life passes us by. The following is an example of what I mean.

Let's say you have a fight with a family member who calls you terrible names, threatens you, and then walks away. There is no resolution to the fight, and so your feelings about it are difficult to change. You might calm yourself down by using ten-by-ten breathing (as we discussed on page 34), then perhaps through saying some positive affirmations and prayer, but the bond between you and this person has been damaged. Whenever you think about the fight, these bad feelings return. And when this is happening, you're living in the past. Therefore, the next time you're with this person, those feelings will color your perception of that person and put you on the defensive.

Some spiritual writers feel the need to distinguish between feelings and emotions: feelings are the here-and-now responses; and emotions are the unresolved feelings. Emotions, from this perspective, are feelings from the past. When we have similar feelings in the present, the emotions can be triggered, adding to the intensity of our affective experience. While I'm not entirely comfortable using the terms "feelings" and "emotions" in this manner, I think the distinction and the realities they indicate are crucial. In the case of the situation of the fight with the family member referred to previously, we could then say that if you are again abused in the same way, you will experience both feelings (current) in addition to emotions (from the past). If there's no safe place to express all of this energy (usually there isn't), you will probably try to suppress this negative energy. You may even build up a network of inner defenses in order to keep it from surfacing at all, thus creating a feeling of numbness.

I have seen ample evidence of these dynamics in the years I worked with chemically dependent people and their families. I have also discovered that even though I do not come from such a family, I have also done the same thing in my life. I, too, had unresolved emotions from childhood, defenses that were built up to keep me safe from them, and, often, I have felt the emotional numbness that arose as a consequence. I had developed a self-concept based, in part, on those experiences. All of this had kept a part of me locked in the past; I was stuck there because of those unresolved emotions, especially shame, resentment, and fear.

It is most likely that every human being lives in a similar situation, for living with unresolved emotions seems to be one of the consequences of living in a world marked by conditional love.

But how do we get out of this vicious circle? We have to let go of the past. The way to do this is through practicing forgiveness.

THE WAY OF FORGIVENESS

To forgive means to emotionally forget. This is not quite the same as that old saying, "to forgive is to forget." Sometimes, we just can't forget what has happened; blocking something out of our memory is impossible unless it has been repressed. Yet we can remember painful events in our lives without getting upset over them. We can say, "Yes, that happened, and it was a very difficult time. I don't ever want to go through that again! Thank God I'm free from that pain."

To free ourselves from our emotional past, we will need to be open to encountering hurtful memories, and maybe even re-experiencing them. However, I don't believe you need to go out looking for encounters with past hurts. If you're going to go through life being here now in love, then, eventually, the psychological obstacles to this spiritual stance will weaken, and the interior incompatibilities will begin to be transformed. The Holy Spirit will take charge of the timing and intensity of what Father Thomas Keating, a Cistercian monk and founder of Contemplative Outreach, has come to call this *"unloading of the unconscious."* Here, in this context, unloading refers to the emergence of old injuries. The purpose is to purge the soul of its inner toxins. At times, specific memories may accompany the unloading process. Sometimes, you may experience certain emotions without knowing the reason why. The important thing to realize is that this re-experiencing is a good thing. Even though you might hurt for a while, this pain is an indication that a deep and essential healing is taking place.

Forgiveness means letting go of those old memories and feelings, letting them pass through your life without identifying with any of them. They are no longer who you are, no matter how significant they may have been in forming your self-concept or moving your life in a particular direction. You can choose an attitude to adopt in order to be able to handle them: you can actually welcome them, allow them to retell their story, cry along (if need be), and then bid them farewell. You can learn how your life has been affected by past experiences, and begin to see that you don't have to live that way any longer.

What is needed most when encountering painful memories is an attitude by which we *hold nothing against* the perpetrator. This attitude is another component of forgiveness; it is the key to releasing the emotions. By *holding nothing against,*

I do not mean to suggest that you must agree with what happened, or be dishonest about its wrongfulness. You might even decide to reject those who have hurt you, and that's a choice you have a right to make. *Holding nothing against means you wish no harm on the other, no vindictiveness!* In fact, you might even pray for the those who have caused your hurt so that they may come to know a different life. When Jesus tells us to pray for our enemies in the Gospel according to Saint Matthew, he is giving us the key to forgiveness. This wish for no harm to come to them, but for them to be helped, will open your will to God's healing love and cleanse the bitterness from your heart.

This act of *holding nothing against* can be applied to you as well. It's quite common to see that some of the pain in our lives has been caused by our own poor choices, sins, or mistakes. People often "beat themselves up" for that, especially if they've experienced painful consequences as a result. For example, ending a relationship because of frequent wrongdoings can lead to self-judgment and condemnation. You hurt from the loss of the relationship, blame yourself, and become locked in a cycle of grief and shame. Don't do this to yourself! Let it go. Your failure to accord yourself the act of self-forgiveness only guarantees that you will be miserable. There is life after mistakes, sins, and broken relationships, but for this to happen, you must let go of the past. In the kingdom of God, there are no unforgivable sins, except to refuse the grace of the Holy Spirit.

Wait! Maybe you are angry with God, too, for some of what has happened in your life, and for allowing certain things to have taken place? That's OK. The psalms are full of such sentiments, and, as far as we know, none of the psalmists were struck dead by lightning for uttering them! Just tell God how you feel; yell and scream it if you need to! God can take it!

After you're done, ask God for the grace to see things in a different way so you don't hold it against him any further.

Forgiveness is a process. Letting go of emotional pain and holding nothing against another person doesn't happen in one "fell swoop." We do it little by little, discovering, along the way, that we can remember a past hurt and not feel upset by it, or think of someone who has wronged us and not feel vindictive. This process is energized by God's grace. God wants so very much for us to forgive others and ourselves; the gospels are full of examples of lessons in forgiveness.

Above all, forgiveness is a blessing for you! When you get stuck in some part of the forgiveness process, remember how much more alive you felt in the past when you have forgiven. Recognize that holding onto pain and wishing harm onto others, or yourself, only hurts you. You're not really punishing anyone but yourself by hardening your heart. Forgive, let go, live.

PUTTING FORGIVENESS OF PAST HURTS INTO PRACTICE

When emotions from the past arise, just see them for what they are, give them a name, experience them, and then release them by not obstructing their passage: keep a journal about them, yell at them, punch a pillow, or dance!

Make a list of people you feel resentment toward and choose one of them. Why are you angry with him or her? Write a letter to this person, express your anger (you can decide later whether to mail it or not). Explain what has happened, how you felt, and the consequences you have suffered in your life. Let it all flow out of you onto the paper.

After you begin to calm down from this second exercise, enter into prayer, and imagine you are standing before the person for whom you felt (and maybe still feel) resentment. Say to this person, "You hurt me! I've suffered consequences for this. But I release you! I bear no ill-will toward you! I hope you will find peace and goodness in your life." If you can't say this sincerely, do the best you can, asking the Holy Spirit to help you.

Work Steps Eight and Nine of the Twelve Steps to Recovery to deal with the wrongs you have done to others. Step Eight states: "We made a list of all persons we had harmed and became willing to make amends to them all." Make this list, consider people you have hurt, and especially those situations where you still feel guilt or shame. Consider what happened, how you felt, how the other person felt, and the consequences that have come to both of you because of the wrong you've done. In Step Nine, you make direct amends to others except when to do so would injure them unnecessarily. Make phone calls, write letters, or even undertake personal visits to apologize, make restitution, or do whatever you need to in order to try to make things right. It doesn't matter if the other person won't accept your efforts; what matters is that you do your part.

If you are a Catholic, go to confession (the sacrament of reconciliation). This is a marvelous opportunity to unburden yourself of your sins and your feelings about them, and receive reassurance of God's forgiveness.

QUIT DEFINING YOURSELF

Sometime in the late seventies, I attended a football game between Louisiana State University and Southern Cal. It was a close game, it went down to the last few seconds and Southern

Cal pulled it out because of a penalty by LSU as well as some great running by Charles White of Southern Cal. Walking out of that stadium, I was so angry at Southern Cal. "We" came so close to beating them, *and they were ranked Number One in the country*! A fellow LSU fan yelled, "Who was for Southern Cal?" A young man yelled back, "I was, and we beat you!" A fight between the two men broke out. If the other LSU fan hadn't reached him first, I would have punched him myself! That's pretty sick, isn't it?

In this section, we'll learn how and why things like this happen, as well as how to begin to free ourselves from the tyrannical aspects of self-concept.

WHAT IS A SELF-CONCEPT?

What image do you have of yourself? When someone asks, "Tell me about yourself," what do you say?

Generally, when people ask this question, we begin by telling them about our job, our marital status, how many children we have, and so forth. We might also make some reference to the fact that we think we are smart, pretty, wealthy, and so on. In short, we externalize certain aspects of our self-concept.

What does the term self-concept *mean?* It is the inner conception, or image, you have of yourself that is a consequence of your experiences in life. Modern psychology has done a great deal to help us understand how it is formed, and how much emotional trouble a negative, or unhealthy, self-concept can cause. Generally, one of the goals of psychotherapy is to help people develop a healthy, or positive, self-concept. There are countless books about this very subject in the self-help or psychology sections of bookstores, and many contain very good advice.

With respect to the spiritual life, however, there are two major considerations which must be taken into account when speaking about self-concept. The first is that *the self-concept is not the Self*; it is only an inner image of the Self that the mind has formed. The second is that *you do not need a positive self-concept to be happy*. It is true that a negative self-concept is correlated with emotional turmoil, but it is certainly not true that you cannot be happy as long as you have a negative self-concept.

An old story recounts that when the Master was asked what it felt like when he became enlightened, he replied: "Before enlightenment, I was depressed. After enlightenment, I was still depressed, but I knew that it was not who I really was, and so I let it go. Then the depression began to disappear and I was freed of it." That is what can happen with spiritual practice.

I use the terms *self-concept* and *self-image* almost interchangeably, even though they are not exactly the same thing. Self-concept is connected to your beliefs about yourself, and self-image is the inner picture of yourself. The image is related to your beliefs, however; change one and you change the other.

We begin to develop ideas about who we are at a very early age. Not only do we have experiences, but we get a sense of how we feel and exist in those experiences, and our memory retains this. As we continue to interact with people, the world, and even our own emerging bodily and psychological powers, we add to this memory of how we feel, how we are, how we react. It is important to recognize that *self-concept is not just the information about our experiences, but how we are in them.* Connecting our memories to one another is this ineffable sense of a human subject, a "me," who is present in, and through, all these experiences. This "me" or "I" is the Ego we hear about in psychology, and the self-concept gives it "form" or its identity. When the "I" is so married to the self-concept, we say that the Ego is a "Mental Ego," meaning that the "I" knows itself largely in terms of its self-concept or image.

Although the self-concept is a very complex system of memories and beliefs, much of its information comes from the following sources:

1. *Roles in life:* father, mother, counselor, husband: all those functions which call forth clusters of behaviors, and give me a sense of how my talents can be used.

2. *Labels:* American, Cajun, Catholic, LSU Tiger fan: descriptions which tell something about who I am.

3. *Self-judgments:* pretty, ugly, smart, slow, pious, sinner, healthy, sick: all those things that seem to put me into a box.

4. *My judgments about other people:* same as above, only it is internalized from what others have said or done in judgment.

Take away these and our self-concept hasn't got much going for it!

SELF-CONCEPT AND JUDGMENT

When we live in the Mental Ego state, the mind is constantly referring back to the self-concept in order to project probable outcomes, and also to integrate our experiences. Suppose, for example, someone asks you to attend a ballet class. You consider what kinds of behaviors a ballet class requires, compare it with your inner picture of yourself, and judge how closely they fit. If they don't quite fit, then you will probably decline.

Yet if your friend's judgment of you and your abilities matters a great deal, then you will decide to go. If the inner image of you isn't too far off, however, and you think it might be good to add these new experiences, then you will probably sign up. This same process goes on, day after day, on a largely unconscious level. The mind makes reference to our self-concept much like a computer software program does to the operating system on which it is running. Without a self-concept, it is nearly impossible for a mind, operating in the Mental Ego stage of development, to make judgments.

You can already see how self-concept leads to judgments by influencing the kinds of decisions you make. But an even more insidious consequence of living out from a self-concept is comparing yourself to others. This, too, happens automatically. You see someone else who has something, or who manifests certain qualities, and your mind makes reference to your self-concept in order to evaluate how it must respond. If these qualities seem to be superior to, or more advanced, than you are, then you will probably judge yourself to be inferior; if not, you will feel superior. In either case, you will be relating to the other through this dynamic of comparison, making it very difficult to know the real person.

When one aspect of our self-concept is threatened, the mind interprets this to be a dangerous situation and activates the fight-or-flight response. For example, let's say you're strongly identified with the label "Catholic," and you have strong, positive judgments about yourself because you belong to this religion. During breaktime at work, a coworker begins to criticize the Catholic Church, saying things you know aren't true. More than likely, you will feel anger toward this person. Why? Because his words launch an assault on a treasured part of your self-concept, your mind interprets him as a threat, activating the fight-or-flight mechanism. That's what happened to me at that LSU–Southern Cal game I mentioned at the beginning of this chapter. "I" was part of the LSU football team (by extension), and if "we" did well, then "I" was fine! Absurd? Yes, but we do it all the time!

SPIRITUALITY AND SELF-CONCEPT

We cannot help having a self-concept; the mind created it before we knew what was happening. We are not primarily responsible for how the deepest layers of our self-concept were formed. Many of the roles we play, the labels to which we are attached, and the judgments we reach about ourselves were infused into our minds at a very early age, and so, for better or worse, we"re "stuck" with them!

What we can begin to do, however, is to see self-concept for what it is, and see how it affects our lives. For example, we will see

- how certain threats to our self-concept activate the fight-or-flight response
- how projecting our self-concept into situations leads to preconceptions about how things will go
- how self-judgments and others' judgments affect the way we feel about ourselves
- how comparing ourselves to others stimulates our emotions

This kind of self-examination is essential for us to grow in self-knowledge. Without it, our self-concept continues to operate on an unconscious level, running our lives for us, simply reinforcing old patterns of behavior. Becoming more aware of how thinking, feelings, behavior, and self-concept interrelate, is, in itself, a freeing practice.

Certain practices in psychology advocate this same kind of self-awareness, but primarily in the interest of modifying our self-concept, turning it to a more positive and socially adapted stance. For example, if you discover that you judge yourself harshly because you are overweight, psychotherapy would encourage you to stop doing this and simply accept yourself the way you are. The same is true for other kinds of emotional turmoil caused by negative conditioning. You can change the programming of the self-concept, but this is a very difficult task, since some of our deepest convictions come from early childhood experiences, which have their roots firmly planted in the deep unconscious.

Spirituality can only be enhanced by this work, for the healthier the self-concept, the less emotional turmoil in the psyche. However, spirituality takes things a step further by reminding us that the self-concept is not really the Self. *The Self, or "I," is a mysterious spiritual reality that cannot really be defined, for it is an image of God, who is ultimately undefinable.* This does not mean that the "I" is unreal, just that it is infinitely more than its inner reflection or concept in the psyche.

When we realize that "*I am, but I am not my self-concept*," and begin to experience the immediacy of the presence of Self, we also begin to loosen our attachment to our self-concept. All sorts of wonderful possibilities then begin to open up, many of which complement the workings of psychology to improve the self-concept. For one thing, I quit defining myself in terms of my labels and roles, for they are not me, but only beliefs I have and things I do. I also quit judging myself, for what is being judged is my self-concept. It is being held up against some kind of ideal, neither of which is really me. I can judge my behavior as good or bad, helpful or not, and the like, and I can resolve to change my behavior, but I am beginning to realize that *I am not my behavior*. I am responsible for it, but *who I am as a person is a mysterious, here and now presence, which exists before I choose to do anything or believe anything.* We will say more about this True Self later on, but, for now, we will simply acknowledge that awakening to its existence goes far beyond the goal of modern psychology.

The moment that we say "This is who I am" we stop growing, even when we attach ourselves to a positive belief (unless it is "I am a mysterious, undefinable child of God"). *Self-concept does not tell us who we really are, but how we have been conditioned.* To define yourself in terms of this conditioning is an illusion, and a source of great unhappiness! Jesus says that to find ourselves we must lose ourselves. Letting go of our self-concept as the primary source of our identity is an essential step in this right direction.

PRACTICING SEPARATION OF YOUR SELF FROM YOUR SELF-CONCEPT

The following is a guide to help you. Contemplate and answer the following statements:

1. *Identify a role that you play every day which has given you a strong sense of who you are.* In your imagination, see yourself acting in this role and then say, "This role is something I do. I am not this role. I am more than this role. This role is an opportunity to be here now in love with these people, and to consider them in a certain way. That is all."

   Do this same exercise with other roles, then with some of the labels you have become attached to (using the word "label" instead of "role" in your affirmations).

2. *Consider some of the judgments you have made about yourself.* Pick one, either positive or negative, and say: "I am both this judgment and its opposite. I have both within me. But I am not either. I simply am."

3. *Now consider some of the judgments others have made about you.* Do the same exercise as you did above about judging yourself.

4. *Avoid adding to the self-concept through the process of identification.* To counter this when you have these feelings, say to yourself: *I feel* (add your feeling word here), *but I am not this feeling. I have this feeling; it is happening inside me; I must choose how to express it. But I am not this feeling.* Do the same with your beliefs, memories, desires, affirming that you have these inner experiences and are responsible for what you do with them, but they do not define you. They are happening within you, so let them tell their stories and learn what you can from them without judging them, or yourself, with respect to them.

POSITIVELY CONNECT THE MIND AND THE SPIRIT

In her autobiography *Collision with the Infinite*, Suzanne Segal, a spiritual author and retreat leader who struggled for ten years to find a context for her loss of self within spiritual traditions, describes her experience of the divine by literally displacing her self and occupying the center of her being. While some might think this to be a wonderful development, Suzanne did not experience it that way. In the absence of her old sense of self, her mind turned the experience into something very negative, a pathology of sorts, and gave the signal that she was in danger. Consequently, she lived in a state of fear for over twelve years, going through a long string of counselors who also viewed her situation as an aberration. It was not until she met a spiritual teacher who understood what had happened to her, and who helped her begin to view it in a positive light, that her fear began to diminish.

Once again, in this book, we note the power the mind has to shape our emotional reality and either open or close our spirit. How we interpret or understand something makes all the difference in the world. *It's not so much what happens to us that makes us feel a certain way, but how we judge or evaluate what happens.* Hence, the importance of living in acceptance, or with a nonjudgmental attitude, as we noted previously. This information is especially important when considering the spiritual journey; how the mind understands what is happening along the way can make the difference between giving consent to grace and openness to the divine, or withdrawing fearfully into self-concern and control.

THE LIFE-GIVING POWER OF THEOLOGY

A classical definition of theology states that it is reason reflecting on faith. Theology might make use of philosophy and other sciences, but without faith, it loses its life-giving power, its heart. When we read a theological text, then, we are not just reading about concepts and ideas; we are also encountering the faith that is expressed through those concepts and ideas. In this way, theology helps to mold the mind and heart to an openness to grace and consent to God's will.

Let us consider the events in first-century Christianity as an example of how theology happens. Jesus had come and walked the earth, dying and arising to new life, and then sending the blessing of the Holy Spirit to form the Church and continue his work on earth. Believing in these events, joining the Church, and accepting the Spirit into one's life is surely the heart of Christian faith, and this was apparently enough knowledge for many people. But there were others who raised questions, some of which addressed this faith and invited it to expand and understand itself better:

— Who was this Jesus? Was he human? divine?
— Why did he have to die as he died?
— What was accomplished by his death?
— What do we mean when we say he rose from the dead?
— Where is Jesus now? What is he doing?
— How does one come to share in the merits gained by Jesus?
— Does one have to first become a Jew to be a Christian?
— What happens to those who die without becoming a Christian?

Some of these questions are more practical than theoretical in their significance, but they are all important, and require thought-out responses that deeply affected the manner in which Christianity was lived. Furthermore, there were a few responses which seemed to lead people away from the faith, and this problem needed to be dealt with as well.

Now, at the beginning of the twenty-first century, Christianity has built up an enormous body of beliefs, many of which come to us in doctrines that are solemnly promulgated by Church councils. Looking up a standard reference, the *Catechism of the Catholic Church*, I see that it's about 1.5 inches thick—and this is a *summary* of Catholic teaching! My *Jerome Biblical Commentary* is over two inches thick, and it's a seven-by twelve-inch book! Even the Bible, which is sitting on my bookshelf, is a formidable read. Do we really have to learn all that is contained in those books to live a spiritual life?

No, of course not! We're not all called to be professional theologians, or Scripture scholars, but we ought to learn as much as we can. It's all *knowledge about* God and the spiritual life, but it could, very well, help us grow more deeply into a *knowledge of* God. This distinction between *knowledge about* and *knowledge of* sums up the difference between religion and spirituality. Theology is the bridge that connects the two. Theology translates the *knowledge of* God, which is acquired through faith, into *knowledge about* God, which can lead the reader to his or her own *knowledge of* God. That, at least, is what good theology is supposed to do. Doctrines are theological convictions considered essential for Christian living, so it's especially important to learn what they have to say.

THEOLOGY AND THINKING ABOUT GOD

Although God is neither a concept nor an idea, nor especially an object of any kind which can be grasped by the mind, how we think about God has a profound influence upon how we relate to God. *Theology helps us formulate an intellectual understanding of who God is and how God acts*, and this understanding can help to move us to consent to God's grace in our lives. One of the reasons Jesus came to earth was to reveal the true nature of God to us in a way we could understand, in a human form. This revelation, and the truths which flow from it, help us to become intellectually oriented to the ways of God.

At the Heartland Center for Spirituality, in Great Bend, Kansas, where I now work, I have occasion to dine with many of the older religious sisters. One of them, Sister Teresita, taught theology for years. She tells a story about how some of the sisters she taught in formation, years ago, used to complain about having to learn theology. "Why," they would ask, "do we need to do this? Why can't we just pray, and serve God?" She would reply, "Because, the more you know about God, the more reasons there are for loving him." This is another good example of the connection between theology and spirituality.

Of course, we need to take a minute to acknowledge that our ideas and concepts about God can also lead us to have preconceptions about who God is and how he acts. Almost every mystical writer has warned against these preconceived notions, telling us that God is never quite like our ideas. The *via negativa* (negative pathway) in Christian spirituality emphasizes this *nada nada* (not this, not that), and the Zen people speak of our ideas about the Ultimate as fingers which point to the moon. These pointers are two-edged swords: if we don't look where they point, we might miss the moon; but once we see the moon, we realize that it's nothing at all like the finger which points to it. To stand around arguing about the finger, or staring at it as though it were God seems…well, pretty sick, don't you think? And yet, at times, there's an awful lot of this kind of discussion in the Church.

With these "provisos" about fingers and the moon in mind, we can proceed to articulate a spiritual perspective on life that can serve us well when things get rough. Many times on the journey, it has been by the light of theological convictions that I have proceeded, for emotional reality was confusing, and spiritual peace was nowhere to be found. Nevertheless, to hold fast to what the intellect affirms to be true is of the utmost importance, and theology can form the intellect into its own pattern of faith.

FORMING THE MIND AND THE SPIRIT

The formation of the mind is an essential part of learning to be here now in love. As mentioned earlier, it doesn't mean you have to be a scholar. It does mean that you take your questions seriously, do some reading, and study to find the answers. Each and every one of us has different needs in this area. There was a time in my life when I read theological and spiritual works of all kinds. I just couldn't seem to get enough! I was hungry for this kind of information, and needed to feed myself with it. Coming, as I did, from a background in science, I had been strongly indoctrinated into a materialistic, evolutionary, and scientific view of things. How the truths of science related to the truths of faith was a pivotal issue for me. Others may not experience the kind of struggle I had, but each of us must do what is necessary to form the mind.

Even if you don't have much interest in theological issues, I think it's important to learn what your religious tradition teaches, and why. Again and again, I see Christians who are confronted with some scientific truth that supposedly contradicts a teaching of the Church, and they feel stumped by it. One should, at least, learn the basics: what the Church teaches about God, how one comes to know God, how to walk with God, what to do when one falls away from God. Everyone should also learn a little about theodicy, a branch of theology which is concerned with God and the problem of suffering. If this awakens more questions in you, then read on.

Those who begin to journey more deeply into the spiritual life can also benefit greatly by reading about how others have experienced the journey. It has helped me, for example, to know about "dark nights," those times when God seems to disappear, but which really signal a new closeness to God. The example from the life of Suzanne Segal cited on page 84 is a case in point. Knowing what contemplative prayer is, and how to consent to its presence has been helpful to me in my growth and in my work. Some of the people I meet with in spiritual direction had been refusing this gift for years, thinking they ought to persevere in their spiritual reading, reflections, and prayers of petition during devotional times. We are not the first to travel the spiritual road, we have brothers and sisters who have gone before us and left blessings of wisdom born out of experience in their writings. Indeed, some of my closest "friends" are saints and mystics who died centuries ago! I feel a bond of closeness to them because of their writings and believe we are, somehow, really connected in God's kingdom.

PUTTING SPIRITUAL FORMATION INTO PRACTICE

Here are some ways to follow a path of spiritual formation.

1. *What are your questions about God, human nature, creation, and the meaning in life?* Make a list of them in your journal, and don't be ashamed. Your questions are your questions, and they could well be grace-filled invitations to grow in faith.

2. *Write out your creed: what you believe about God, human nature.* Read it over from time to time, and update it as needed.

3. *If you haven't already done so, learn what your religious tradition teaches.* Get a catechism, or a compendium of teachings, and read a little of it each day. All of it might not be personally relevant, but knowing what's there might be helpful.

4. *Study the Bible.* It's one thing to pray with Scripture to encounter the living God through the Word, but another to learn the "objective" meaning of Scripture. Scripture, first and foremost, means what the author intended it to mean. To be able to know this meaning, you need to understand the cultural, historical, spiritual, and linguistic factors that prompted the writings. There are good books to help you study the Bible to gain this understanding. Get one and begin to learn a little each day.

5. *Be open to attending lectures, retreats, workshops and courses on theology and spirituality.* Give one a try sometime.

ENCOUNTER THE FOUR MODES OF CHRIST'S PRESENCE

In the past, when I have given workshops and retreats on the theme "Be Here Now in Love," participants sometimes complain that this spiritual approach isn't sufficiently Christ-centered. After all, you don't have to be a Christian to be here now, or to love. One young man even accused me of teaching Buddhism.

It is certainly true that you don't have to be a Christian to be here now in love. Anyone can do that, and I'm sure the God of love is quite happy when we do so. But what is also true is that a person can be a committed Christian and also not be focused on this kind of spirituality. What is best, I am convinced, is when the Christian faith is brought into this kind of spiritual approach to living. We've touched on this before in previous sections and have, all along, encouraged prayer for guidance about how to respond in the moment, or discern what's next, and so forth. Now, I am going to discuss the four modes of Christ's presence, with special emphasis on how we encounter Christ when we are lovingly present to life.

MEET THE PERSONAL, HISTORICAL JESUS

For most Christians, it is the personal, historical Jesus who is at the core of their faith. When they think of Christ, in their minds, they are thinking of Jesus, the man, the person who walked this earth more than two thousand years ago, teaching, healing, suffering, dying, and rising from the dead. They also might have images representing him in their home, or a crucifix, or some other reminder of his life and all it communicated to us about God.

The personal, historical Jesus is someone with whom we can be in relationship. Because he was human, we feel we can talk with him because he understands our situation; we can focus on him and experience a bond of love developing between us. Through faith, we know that he still lives, and also that this man, who once existed in space and time with a body like ours, is, somehow, still available to us in his risen state. His manner of life, now, is radically different from ours, but we believe that all of his memories of what human life was like have been preserved. Jesus did not stop being human when he rose from the dead and ascended to heaven. For this reason, we have someone who is able to understand our human situation, for he experienced it in every way that we do, although he did not sin (see Heb 4:15).

How do we come to know the historical Jesus? There are many avenues for doing so, including exposure to movies, books, paintings, statues, preaching, and teaching about him. The best way, however, is to prayerfully study his life as it is presented to us in the gospels. Here, while we see him going about doing good and revealing to us the inner heart of God, in the process, something of his presence is communicated to us. We find that we are not merely reading a story, but we are encountering a person. That very same Jesus of Nazareth who once walked the earth, now comes to us through the Gospel, inviting us into relationship with him. Our minds and hearts are "warmed" by him, invited to draw closer, and even inspired to become disciples. Eventually, we come to a moment of decision: will we say "yes" to him? This may happen to us many times, each occasion inviting us to a deeper knowledge of Jesus.

Through our knowledge of the personal, historical Jesus, we come to know the personal God, whom Jesus called "Father." We come to see that faith is more than an adherence to a system of beliefs or living by principles; it is a relationship with a Person. It appears that, without this kind of relationship with Jesus, the other modes of encountering him lose some of this "relational" quality. Coming to know Jesus as one's Lord, savior, brother, and friend is a wonderful possibility opened to us by the grace of Christian faith.

MEET JESUS THROUGH THE CHURCH

Although it isn't always recognized as such at first, for most people, the Church is the place where they experience their most tangible encounter with Jesus. They are a part of a living, vibrant, church community and experience a sense of renewed life from the experience. *Those people have something*, they might think to themselves. Or, as the pagans said about the early Church: "See how they love one another!" The community shows hospitality, love, concern, and even compassion! Eventually, the visitor comes to know the source of these graces, but it is doubtful if they will get that far without the support of the community.

After Jesus ascended to heaven, he sent the Holy Spirit to continue his work on earth through the Church. This is not to say that he is not working in other religions as well, just that it seems his main intention was to found a Church that would consciously and intentionally invite the Spirit to train its members and do his work. Through this Church, he multiplied his presence. Where once he was one man, going about doing good, he now lives in millions of people, who constitute his Mystical Body.

This understanding of the Church as being Christ's presence was forcibly drawn to Saint Paul's attention. As he traveled the road to Damascus in search of Christians to arrest and persecute, the glorified Christ intervened, striking him blind and speaking to him: " 'Saul, Saul, why do you persecute me?' He [Paul] asked, 'Who are you, Lord?' The reply came, 'I am Jesus, whom you are persecuting' " (Acts 9:4–5). Earlier in his life, Jesus had taught his disciples, "Where two or three are gathered in my name, I am there among them" (Mt 18:20). Now, with his message to Paul, he left no doubt that he was intimately identified with his Church.

It is possible to have Christian faith without belonging to a Church, but it doesn't make much sense. Christ made it clear that the Church was his Mystical Body, that he wanted us to gather in his name to worship, to celebrate the Eucharist, and to bring the Good News to the ends of the earth. When we exclude ourselves from Church, we miss this mode of his presence, and the accompanying formative graces given there that enable us to recognize him in other areas of life as well. No Church is perfect, however. Christ continues to suffer in his Mystical Body as we struggle in the Church to bring our fallen redeemed brothers and sisters into conformity with his will.

MEET CHRIST IN THE SACRAMENTS

A traditional understanding of the term "sacrament" explains that it is a sign, instituted by Christ, to give grace. In many ways, then, the Church is the first sacrament of Christ, since it is a visible sign of his presence, and a means through which his grace is given. The Church is also the living context in which other sacramental experiences take place, some of which are formally designated to call to mind Christ's presence in special ways. All Christian denominations recognize baptism as a sacrament of initiation into a new life in Christ and membership in the Church (the term "sacrament," however, is not used by all). Many others also celebrate the Eucharist, although there are differences among them concerning the nature of Christ's presence there. In addition, churches in the Catholic tradition recognize matrimony, confirmation, penance, holy orders, and the anointing of the sick as sacramental experiences.

One of the primary purposes of the sacraments is to help us realize that Christ is with us during those special times and rites of passage in our life. His self-communication through a sacramental mode speaks to our ordinary, human modes of knowing, but it also invokes symbols that point beyond the literal into transcendence. For example, we understand that water is commonly used as a means of quenching our thirst and as a cleansing agent. When it is used in baptism, we intuitively understand that just as water cleanses a body, so, too, does Christ cleanse the soul, and that he is the Living Water who will now quench our deepest thirst. The water used is ordinary, but it points to the Living Water, which is the extraordinary. Likewise, bread and wine broken and shared in the Eucharist maintain their appearance, but communicate now the Body and Blood of Christ. A married couple show love to each other, and this signifies the love between Christ and the Church. And so forth.

With respect to the spiritual life, we can say that the sacraments help train us to look beyond the literal to a deeper reality. They do not reject the literal, or ordinary, modes of human knowledge; the forms used in sacraments are not merely incidental, but essential. But they do lead us to be open to other modes of encountering Christ beyond those which are familiar to the senses and the concepts of the mind. They are like windows into the spiritual realm: we can look through them and find Christ looking back, and, if we open the windows by receiving the sacraments in faith, we can be refreshed by the breath of his Spirit.

A final observation is that it seems that contemplative spirituality flowers most in those Christian denominations which hold an appreciation for the sacraments. Those religious that do not have these kinds of experiences certainly manifest a love for the personal, historical Christ and his Spirit, and that is good. But I am convinced that Christ wants us to know him more fully through these sacramental means, which is why, even in the first century of Christianity, we see the beginnings of these celebrations which we are still privileged to experience.

MEET CHRIST IN THE COSMOS

Earlier in this section, we mentioned that the personal, historical Christ is the very one who rose from the dead and ascended to heaven. The human Jesus did not go away, but he was certainly radically transformed, now living in a glorified state that preserves his humanity while integrating it fully into divinity. In the prologue to Saint John's Gospel, and through the teachings of the Church, we learn that Jesus was the incarnation of the Word, or the Second Person of the Trinity. It was through this Word that God the Father and Creator made all things

(1:3). All of creation is, thus, intimately joined with God through the Word. In the case of Jesus, the Word gave him a human form: Jesus had a human soul as we do, and he still possesses that soul. But he was different from us because the Word also become incarnate with his conception. The human soul of Jesus and the Word were so intimately joined that it was impossible to separate one from the other: he was not a human being with a divine nature superimposed, but a man who was *simultaneously* 100 percent human *and* 100 percent divine. We don't, and can't, fully understand how this works, but through the spiritual journey, something of the same happens to us as well, since our human nature is transformed by grace. In Christ's case, this transformation was not necessary, for he was already fully one with the divine.

In his historical human body, the presence of Jesus could be isolated to a specific place in space and time, as is the case for all of us. We are here, but not there, in one place, but not another. When he rose from the dead and ascended into heaven, however, his human soul become fully integrated into the Word with whom it was already united. One might ask, "Where is this Word?" It is at the heart of all created things as its Source and Center. Its body is the universe and all its parts, and so that is where Jesus can be found as well (see Col 1:15–17).

What this means, then, is that all of reality is, in fact, sacramental, a symbolic means through which Christ is present to us. It may be more difficult to find him in a tree or a rock than in the bread and wine shared in a vibrant liturgy, but he is, nonetheless, present to us through all creation. The Church's sacraments help us to learn to be open to this mystical, cosmic dimension of Christ's presence, while our knowledge of him, through the Church and Scripture, enables us to recognize that it is, indeed, the same presence in creation we encountered in the other modes of knowing. Marvel of marvels! We discover that Jesus is lovingly present to us through everything, all the time! We don't have to be in a church or read a Bible to meet him. All we need is to be here now in love, for that is where he is and that is what he is doing.

These days, there are many who fear that this emphasis on the Cosmic Christ might lead people away from the Church or to other, nonacceptable practices. I hope, however, that I have sufficiently emphasized how important it is to know him in all of these four modes. The Eastern Christian Churches have long recognized the mystical, cosmic dimension of Christ without losing their appreciation for his presence in the Church, the sacraments, and Scripture. Meanwhile, the churches of the West, with their emphasis placed on dogma, ritual, and service, have lost much of this cosmic mysticism. It is there for us to claim; Christ is still present in everything, just waiting for us.

This understanding of the Christ in the cosmos also helps us to begin to comprehend something about how other kinds of religious experiences might happen. What if, for example, spiritual seekers who knew nothing of the historical, personal Jesus, or his Church and its sacraments, co-operated with the moral and spiritual instincts God has created within us, and came to an awakening of the Ultimate Reality as the Ground of their own being and everything else that exists? This would surely be an experience of Christ in his cosmic aspect, but, lacking the assistance of Christian revelation and a life in the Church, it might not be understood or even experienced in the same way as those who have known Christ in all four modes. There are many implications, here, for interreligious dialogue, but that is not the focus of this work. Nevertheless, it has helped me to find and awaken to a new closeness with my brothers and sisters in other world religions. We all do worship that same God, even the same Christ, only we know him in different ways.

PUTTING ENCOUNTERS WITH JESUS INTO PRACTICE

Ask yourself the following questions:

- Which of the modes of knowing Christ is most meaningful to you? Which is least meaningful?
- What do you need to do to meet Christ in each of the modes?
- How do you experience Christ in the practice of being here now in love?

THE AWAKENING OF TRUE SELF

Many years ago, even long after beginning the spiritual journey, I would, occasionally, experience interior silence, but I found it boring, so I didn't stay there very long. I thought the point of the spiritual life was to have edifying thoughts, loving feelings, and a strong resolution to change the world. My prayer at that time in life was largely discursive (*kataphatic*), consisting of reading, thinking, asking for an intercession, and the like. This practice "fired me up" to promote the Gospel and launched me on a career as a lay minister. As long as that kind of activity was going on in my head, it was easy to evaluate the contents of my consciousness and reassure myself that I was really "doing something" for God.

As the years went by, this kind of interior activity began to subside, causing me to wonder if I still had the same evangelical zeal. I had read about contemplative prayer, but figured this type of prayer was just for the professed religious, or really holy people. It never occurred to me that my inclination to a more silent form of prayer was really a call to contemplative spirituality. Further, I had no spiritual director at that time to nudge me in this direction. I found myself just enjoying sitting in God's presence and being "warmed," as it were, by love. Even though my mind was not very active, I knew God was communicating with me and I felt more alive deep inside than ever before. At the same time, I also felt confused, however, for with the slowing of my thoughts, it seemed that my identity was also fading and I was losing clarity about how to serve God. Finally, I found a spiritual director, an ex-Trappist, who told me I was awakening to my True Self. Naturally, I was excited to hear this, but then I made the usual mistake and tried to define what the True Self was, creating a concept of it in my mind, and then "trying" to act accordingly. Well, there went the silence, and the beautiful, deep sense of union with God. I read books by Thomas Merton, Bernadette Roberts, Thomas Keating, and almost anyone who had anything to say about contemplation and the self. This helped to validate my experience somewhat, but it also aggravated my tendency to create a "True Self concept" and live that. Finally, my spiritual director told me to stop reading about it and to just go back to praying. I could read anything I wanted, as long as it had no relation to spiritual identity.

It worked! I began to relax again, my mind became quieter and receptive, and the deep silence began to emerge.

FORGING A SPIRITUAL IDENTITY

My mind did not give its search up completely, however. With the return of the silence and resting, there was a fading of identity, emotional aridity, and a certain "flatness" of the will emerged. In my journals, I recorded that I had lost my affective memory and intentional consciousness. This was quite a loss indeed, when you come to think of it! And yet, there was no denying that life continued in this body, in this person. "Someone" was at home, even if he was not thinking about his sense of self. "I" was there all right, but in an entirely different way. "I" was a mystery, undefined and unable to be defined. "I" had a past, but it could not be explained in those terms. "I" had a self-concept, but that was just how my memory had organized my experiences. "I" had a future and it could be planned, but that was simply "I" using its faculties of reason and intuition in the service of prudence. What "I" was could not be explained. *I simply am*, I told myself. And that is the truth!

One of the things I noticed when I was faced with a problem was that my mind would become active. Just feed a question to the mind, and the computer starts churning. Imbue the question or problem with emotional energy, and the computer starts working nonstop.

With the awakening of this new sense of "I," my mind was becoming silent. It seemed there was nothing to figure out any longer, at least nothing about myself! It is true, I surely had problems, especially financial ones. But if I didn't want my mind to concentrate on that, I could just shift my attention to the reality in this moment and to whatever was in my field of vision, and my mind became quiet. What became obvious was that my mind had mostly lost interest in trying to figure out the mystery of my self. The problem of identity had been solved. "I am here," was the conclusion, and even this was an experience, not merely an intellectual affirmation. In the True Self, there is absolutely no confusion about identity, and no concern about it either.

TRUE SELF AND SMALL SELF

Now, I am convinced that the "problem of identity" is the major cause of much of our mental disquietude or anxiety. The reason is that, early on in life, we encounter a world of non-love, and in order to avoid getting hurt, we recoil within ourselves and develop a set of defenses for self protection. We have noted this circumstance in earlier chapters with respect to forming attachments and the use of quick fixes. Now, we notice that this act of recoiling, and its defense system, give us a sense of being a defined, individual self that is separated from both other people and created things. We experience life within this boundary, and our memory keeps a record of what this self thinks and feels, providing us with our self-concept, or self-image. This, in turn, to a greater extent, helps us feel that we are a separate, solid individual.

The True Self, however, is a direct creation of God, emerging from his creative *fiat* in each and every second of existence. When we contract our will away from loving, this very act creates a distortion in the psyche which prevents us from experiencing this kind of direct contact with God. In our minds, we know we are here, but we experience ourselves as being alienated from God, or, if we know God, it is through the medium of the self-concept which encapsulates the "I." As a result, we have all kinds of indirect experiences of God through the medium of thought, visualization, memory, emotion, and the like. Granted, these are all good and necessary, for they draw attention to our true state of being, but they are always "tainted," as it were, by the contents of our psyche.

PSYCHOLOGY, THE TRUE SELF, AND SPIRITUALITY

Psychological counseling can help heal our inner wounds to a certain extent, but not completely. It is good to move from a negative self-image to a more positive one, to loosen the hold on defenses, and to eliminate negative emotional energy. Total healing does not come, however, until the action of recoiling from life is reversed. Moving a person in this direction is the work of spirituality. Psychology and spirituality can work at this together, "hand in hand." This joint effort is often desirable, but, ultimately, most psychological counselors do not have enough knowledge about the True Self that lies beyond our structures of self-concept and its defenses (certain transpersonal psychologists and those who practice spirituality-based counseling are an exception).

When I speak of reversing the recoil from life as being the major concern of religion, what I am referring to is the movement from selfishness toward love. The inner recoil, which might be considered the major sign of original sin, has us mired in conditionality, with the self convinced that it is only conditionally lovable and acceptable. The mind, in turn, is constantly trying to create the conditions we believe necessary for acceptance, and is scanning the environment to see where these might be present. These are the themes for most mental and emotional disquietude. This is what keeps us from being here now in love.

In order to wake up, we must move out of the whole, sorry mess, and that takes time. It also takes work, lots of hard work! The following are steps in the right direction:

- The recoil must be reversed by striving to love instead of act selfishly. Just looking at God is one of the most important ways we do this.

- The painful emotions of shame, resentment, and fear caused by our recoil from life, and living in a sinful world, must be healed.
- Our self-concept must be seen for what it is, and then the self must "dis-identify" from it.
- Our defenses must be lessened, and then dropped, so we can let life flow in and out.

Every little progress toward any of these end results enables the True Self to shine forth more fully. The result is that we will feel more free, more relaxed, more alive, and this emboldens us to press forward with our work.

THE PRACTICE OF LIVING IN THE TRUE SELF

There is never a time when we are without our True Self. It is always there, yet, sometimes it is "hidden under a bushel basket." In truth, it is the only self we have: anything else we call a self is an illusion, a fabrication of the memory, or a construction of the intellect. The real, living person that God is creating, in each moment, is always there in every moment, and we can see this clearly every time someone reaches out in love, or lets his or her defenses down (be here now in love). You can even see it in people's pain and selfishness if you look close enough, for it can be so distorted we can easily miss it.

The True Self is your experience when you can stand firmly planted in this moment with your mind more silent, your heart open to giving and receiving love, and your intuition discerning what is needed. It is such a simple experience that, even when we come to it, we think it's "no big deal," or, perhaps, even boring! Becoming acclimated to this state of being takes time, and it acts as an accompaniment to the falling away of our small self and its emotional roller coaster. It's a journey, but the fruit can be tasted early on, gradually becoming sweeter and more nourishing as we learn how to live.

The practice of being here now in love is the surest way to help be a midwife to the birth of the True Self, for this is the very attitude of the True Self. The True Self is always here and now, even when it is being attentive to thoughts, memories, and the like.

It is also always loving, although its manner of loving might not fit everyone's definition. In one of his last retreat conferences, Jesuit Father Anthony de Mello described love as being "clarity of perception, accuracy of response." That is how the True Self loves: it sees things as they are, and is spontaneously moved to the correct response. These responses all happen without the necessity of introspection or deliberation: one just "knows" what to do. The mind is free to question this course of action, certainly, but it will never make a better decision than the one that the True Self is moved to make.

In terms of theology, we could say that the True Self is who we are as an "image and likeness" of God. To see someone in the True Self is to see the reflection of God in human form. It is always possible to behold the reflection of the Christ in nature, for nature is pure and undefiled. But to behold this reflection of Christ in another human being is a powerful experience, for the human form more closely approximates the spiritual God than does anything else in nature. Jesus Christ revealed God most fully in human form, and those who live in the True Self have, themselves, become like Christ. This Christ-likeness is the reason we were created, to know God as Christ knows God. The really good news is that we can begin to experience this knowledge during our time on earth, although its fullness will not come until death.

SUMMARY STEPS FOR BEING
HERE NOW IN LOVE

Here is a summary of steps involved in the practice of being here now in love.

- *Bring your attention into the present moment by being where you are and doing what you're doing.* Don't consciously try to force your mind and will, just keep gently drawing your attention back to the present moment, and opening your heart to giving and receiving life.
- *When you become preoccupied about something in the past or future, ask yourself what you can do about it right now.* If the answer is "nothing," then say a prayer, commending the concern to God's care, and then just drop it and bring your attention back to being here now in love.
- *Stay in your "skin," in touch with your lived experience.* Notice all through the day what you're feeling, your body sensations, your inner desires. Get rid of all unnecessary external noises such as radio, TV, and the like, which pull you too far away from your experience.
- *Ask "what's next?" as you go through the day.* Listen within yourself for the answer.
- *Take time each day for formal practices* such as prayer, writing in a journal, spiritual reading, and so forth, which strengthen your mind, focus your will, and facilitate inner healing.

Appendix A

TWELVE STEPS TO RECOVERY

1. We admitted we were powerless over our compulsive behavior—that our lives had become unmanageable.

2. We came to believe that a Power greater than ourselves could restore us to sanity.

3. We made a decision to turn our will and our lives over to the care of God as we understood Him.

4. We made a searching and fearless moral inventory of ourselves.

5. We admitted to God, to ourselves, and to another human being the exact nature of our wrongs.

6. We were entirely ready to have God remove all these defects of character.

7. We humbly asked him to remove our shortcomings.

8. We made a list of all persons we had harmed and became willing to make amends to them all.

9. We made direct amends to such people wherever possible, except when to do so would injure them or others.

10. We continued to take personal inventory and when we were wrong, promptly admitted it.

11. We sought, through prayer and meditation, to improve our conscious contact with God as we understood him, praying only for knowledge of his will for us, and the power to carry that out.

12. Having had a spiritual awakening as the result of these steps, we tried to carry this message to other persons in need of recovery and to practice these principles in all our affairs.

Appendix B

❧

SUGGESTED READING

The selections which follow are recommended because they have all significantly influenced the development of the spirituality articulated in this book. Some may prove to be "more relevant" than others, but they all can provide helpful guidance and support for anyone on a spiritual journey.

Arraj, James. *God, Zen and the Intuition of Being.* Chiloquin, Or.: Inner Growth Books, 1988.

Clément, Olivier. *The Roots of Christian Mysticism.* London: New City, 1995.

de Caussade, Jean Pierre. *Abandonment to Divine Providence.* New York: Doubleday/Image, 1993.

de Mello, Anthony, S.J., *Awareness: A de Mello Spirituality Conference in His Own Words.* New York: Doubleday, 1990.

_____. *The Way to Love: The Last Meditations of Anthony de Mello.* New York: Doubleday, 1995.

Eckhart, Meister. *Meister Eckhart, a Modern Translation.* Raymond B. Blakney (translator). New York: Harper and Row. 1941

Enomiya-Lasalle, Hugo, S.J. *Living in the New Consciousness* (translation). Boston: Random House, 1988.

Finley, James. *The Awakening Call: Fostering Intimacy With God*. Notre Dame, Ind.: Ave Maria Press. 1984.

Goettmann, Alphonse and Rachel. *The Beyond Within: Initiation into Christian Meditation*. St. Meinrad, Ind.: Abbey Press. 1992.

Graham, Dom Aelred. *Zen Catholicism*. New York: Crossroad. 1994.

Greene, Thomas H. *When the Well Runs Dry: Prayer Beyond the Beginnings*. Notre Dame, Ind.: Ave Maria Press, 1979.

_____. *Weeds Among the Wheat: Discernment, Where Prayer and Action Meet*. Notre Dame, Ind.: Ave Maria Press, 1984.

Haught, John F. *The Cosmic Adventure: Science, Religion and the Quest for Purpose*. New York: Paulist Press, 1984.

Johnston, William. *Mystical Theology: The Science of Love*. San Francisco: HarperSF, 1995.

_____, Ed. *The Cloud of Unknowing and The Book of Privy Counseling*. New York: Doubleday-Image, 1973.

Keating, Thomas. *Open Mind, Open Heart: The Contemplative Dimension of the Gospel*. Rockport, Mass.: Element Books, 1991.

_____. *Invitation to Love*. Rockport, Mass.: Element Books., 1992.

Maloney, George. *Uncreated Energy: A Journey into the Authentic Sources of Christian Faith*. Amity, N.Y.: Amity House, 1987.

Manes, Virginia and Mary Frohlich, eds. *The Lay Contemplative: Testimonies, Perspectives, Resources*. Cincinnati, Ohio: St. Anthony Messenger Press, 2000.

May, Gerald. *Will and Spirit: A Contemplative Psychology*. San Francisco: HarperSF, 1987.

_____. *The Awakened Heart: Living Beyond Addiction, Opening Yourself to the Love You Need*. San Francisco: HarperSF, 1993.

Merton, Thomas. *Zen and the Birds of Appetite*. New York: New Directions, 1968.

Nouwen, Henri J. M. *The Way of the Heart*. New York: Ballantine Books. 1981.

Rolheiser, Ronald. *The Holy Longing: the Search for a Christian Spirituality*. New York: Doubleday, 2001.

St. John of the Cross. *Dark Night of the Soul* (Peers translation). New York: Doubleday-Image, 1959.

St. Romain, Philip S. *Caring for the Self, Caring for the Soul: A Book of Spiritual Development*. Liguori, Mo.: Liguori/Triumph, 2000.

Shannon, William H. *Silence on Fire: The Prayer of Awareness*. New York: Crossroad, 2000.